May you walk in His grace

Leona Nichols

2015

OTHER LOVES ALL FLEE

LEONA KOEHN NICHOLS

authorHOUSE®

AuthorHouse™
1663 Liberty Drive
Bloomington, IN 47403
www.authorhouse.com
Phone: 1-800-839-8640

Published by AuthorHouse   12/11/2014

ISBN: 978-1-4969-5782-5 (sc)
ISBN: 978-1-4969-5783-2 (hc)
ISBN: 978-1-4969-5781-8 (e)

Library of Congress Control Number: 2014921903

CONTENTS

FORWARD TO OTHER
LOVES ALL FLEE

Years have passed since many of the events in this story were lived out. Some of the key players in the drama that unfolded have gone to their Eternal Rewards. Some have moved to other communities. In the beginning as we struggled to hold on to our membership, we were encouraged by friends to move away from this area, possibly to another congregation that was less conservative. We felt constrained to stay right where we were, and to live out our faith among the people we had grown up with. We had nothing to hide, nor did we want to run from controversy. We believed with all our heart that God was big enough to keep us walking close to Him no matter where we lived.

It is important for us to state that we have never stopped loving our people and wish only the best for them. We have no ax to grind. Throughout those crucial months, we were treated with dignity and respect, and we made every effort to respond in like fashion. We were well aware of the Apostle Paul's statement that at best we all "see as through a glass darkly." We have no degree in theology nor are our lives focused on proving who is right and who is wrong. We do know that we have different points of view on what it means to be a Christ-follower. And we are so thankful that we are privileged to follow our own convictions.

Our children are now grown, and it has become important for this story to be chronicled for our grandchildren. They have all been brought up in Christian homes but have lived very different lives than we experienced. Not only have times changed, but the legalism that was a part of our lives is no longer in place. However, as in every age, they have their own challenges.

As we live out our remaining years, our goal is the same as that of our parents and grandparents, to accept the free gift of salvation by His grace and to spend eternity with the Savior, whose death on the cross on our behalf gives purpose and meaning to our lives. We are incredibly thankful for the on-going grace and mercy we receive at His hand. Because of His grace, we're forgiven, and we know without a doubt that our future is with the God of the Universe in His heavenly home. Our prayer is that every reader of this book will also choose to receive that blessed hope for themselves. Blessings to each of you as fellow travelers along the way.

COMMENDATION FROM OUR PASTOR:

Willis and Leona Koehn Nichols are those rare individuals where the joy of the Lord really does show in every conversation and encounter. They have been a part of the family at New Life Christian Center almost since our beginning. They have never been spectators or casual attenders, but have been actively involved and connected in every aspect of New Life's call to see people come to a real and authentic faith in Jesus Christ. The vibrancy of their own authentic faith has been an inspiration to me, as well as to our entire church.

Pastor David Larson

New Life Christian Center

A WORD OF THANKS

To give thanks to the many people who have impacted our lives in a positive way would be impossible. However, certain individuals stand out as having been especially encouraging. These I would like to mention by name.

First of all, my husband, Willis, with whom I have shared this journey, and whose insight and kindness have always been a blessing, especially during the most difficult times.

To my three daughters, Micki, Bethany, and Darlisa, all of whom have prayed and encouraged, and whose personal commitment to Jesus is always an inspiration to me.

To my three sons, Bruce, Danny, and Jon, whose love for their mom has given me joy and has encircled me with their tender caring.

And for the many friends who listened, prayed, and encouraged during the hard times. I especially thank friends, Ray and Glenda Eck, who walked through much of this journey with us, and whose prayerful support and knowledge of the Word was fittingly given at just the right time.

And to our pastor, Pastor Dave Larson, whose gift of encouragement extends to the many and diverse members of his flock who depend on the Holy Spirit teaching them through his ministry, week after week. All of these dear ones have impacted my husband's and my walk with the Lord.

I owe a debt of gratitude for the hours my daughter Micki spent in editing and re-editing, catching many of the mistakes I made in this manuscript. Her skill brought clarity in how events and thoughts were expressed. And for Darlisa and husband Tim, who understood the directions and prepared the photo section that gives a glimpse into our family.

Finally, and most of all, to my Lord and Savior, Jesus Christ, who loved me enough to walk with me though the Valley of Misunderstanding that was so much a part of our story. May His name be lifted up and may all men be drawn to Him. Amen.

OTHER LOVES ALL FLEE

Part One

A New Beginning

Chapter One

We walked into the church that Sunday morning, for all appearances just like any other Holdeman Mennonite family in congregations of our denomination across the country. Our six children were neatly dressed in their Sunday best, their faces scrubbed and clean, hair carefully combed, and their Sunday School books clutched in their hands. As parents, we hoped the continuity of familiar patterns would somehow shield the children from the pain which would inevitably follow the knowledge of what had just occurred.

My husband and I made every attempt to maintain our usual composure, our faces carefully controlled as we concealed the misgivings which our new status had created within us. Difficult as it was, we did that morning what we had done every Sunday morning of our lives: attend Sunday morning services. Regular church attendance had been the hub around which our lives had revolved for so many years, and now, on this most stressful of mornings, we did not consider an alternative.

Spring comes early to the Central Valley of California, and already the almond orchards were in full bloom. The delicate, sweet aroma of almond blossoms wafted across the church yard on the early morning breeze. The cycle of seasons which the church families knew so well was beginning again. Winter's austere look with its bare and leafless branches had given way to the lacy look of spring, and the blooming orchards looked especially festive.

The orderly progression of seasons was reassuring to the farm families of our multicultural community. The onset of the new season always symbolized hope. No matter how disappointing the previous harvest or how unstable the market, each year was a fresh opportunity to start over. On this particular February morning, orchards of almonds in full bloom were a reminder that spring was once again holding forth its promise of a new beginning.

In the privacy of our own hearts, my husband and I, reluctantly, yet with a certain objectivity, were also contemplating a new beginning.

1

Everything around us, the landscape, the churchyard dotted with cars, and the church house itself starting to fill with people for the morning service, appeared the same. Only we were different. Nothing, of course, that could be seen on the outside. We wore no scarlet letter, but we felt as conspicuous as though we carried a highly egregious mark of some kind visible upon us. Since the meeting of the previous evening, we were no longer members of the closely knit religious group both our families had belonged to for generations. We felt this diminished status with every fiber of our being.

Neither our parents nor we were familiar with any other life than that of the culture in which we lived. We had little or no contact with "the world," the term used to designate people and practices outside our own people. And now, by the decision of our local congregation, we had been officially excommunicated. We had always supposed that excommunication was the worst thing that could happen. To be judged by those we loved and who loved us as no longer worthy to remain within the fold of the church was the most traumatic experience we could endure. We had lost our membership in the very church that we had been taught was "the one true visible church," the only church whose practices were in accordance with God's plan for His people. We knew the doctrines of the church with its own unique interpretation of the Scriptures. The Old Testament taught that those who were disobedient were to be put outside the camp that they might see the error of their ways. Even in the New Testament, believers were instructed to shun the erring brother. Discipline was to be carried out in love, however, so that the deviant one would be drawn back into the fold. The hope was, if God should then extend His grace on their behalf, they might find forgiveness upon their earnest efforts to repent.

Of all the conflicting emotions we struggled with that morning, regret that it had come to this mingled with relief that it was finally over. We had not been able to resolve our differences with the leadership of the church we had grown up in, though we had tried for nearly two years, and physically and emotionally we needed the respite from pressure. These differences had culminated in our excommunication, a word that had such connotations of shame that I would never had been able to link it with our family in earlier years. Yet, it appeared, we would survive. The peace that enveloped us as we walked into the familiar building seemed supernatural. It had nothing to do with whether we were right or wrong, whether the charges against us were true or false, or even whether we might be able to find a way to adjust to our status as outcasts. This peace was much deeper than that and had little to do with the circumstances in which we found ourselves. At the very foundation of our lives, we had come to a deep-seated conviction that, regardless of supposed evidence to the contrary, we were loved. In the trauma of this most difficult severance from all that was familiar and dear, one belief emerged again and again—God loved us. Just as we were, stripped of our status, emptied of all our self-righteous arrogance, and devoid of our good works, He loved us. In the painful months we had just passed through, as we found ourselves re-examining our familiar dogmas, we felt ourselves to be standing naked before God. So many unanswered questions filtered through our minds. But, even then, our spirits were bathed in the warmth of an unreasoning, incomprehensible love.

The first burgeoning evidence of this concept of unconditional love had emerged a few years earlier when I had finally grown to a place where I could examine my own faith. It came to light in an essay I had written to acquaint myself with my own feelings. I had called it "The Search," and in it I had explored my concept of the God of my childhood. In the course of my discovery, I had written that Creator God, for whatever purpose or intent, had created me to be human, and that I was, by that very creative act, also fallible. And since it was God who made me fallible, it was no surprise to Him when I failed. It was as basic to my character as infallibility was to His. Therefore, He was not shocked or angry when I was less than perfect.

As simple as this thesis is, it was life-changing for me, for it follows naturally that, this being the case, His love was not and is not contingent upon my performance. What a revelation that had been for me that day, and now, on this day when a part of my world seemed to end, this truth enveloped me like a warm cocoon of love. We, my husband, myself, and our children, were free to make mistakes—He still loved us. Better than a dishonest parroting of dogma we did not hold to be true, we could express our honest doubts and know that He still loved us. In fact, more than any other principle we held to, amidst the confusion that encircled us, was the conviction that we must be honest. Honestly wrong seemed better than dishonestly right, if that were possible. If we were honest with ourselves and before God, then honesty would become a path that could lead us to a fuller understanding and revelation of truth.

We believed this with our whole hearts. As a child, I had often jumped into the outstretched arms of my father when I had climbed to some high place and couldn't get down. Now we were releasing ourselves from a place that had lost its security into the outstretched, loving arms of a Heavenly Father. Certainly there were uncertainties, but there was also great confidence that His arms were strong enough to catch us and keep us safe.

How had we come to such a place? Over and over we retraced our steps to discover why we, of all families, should have reached this crucial point. Certainly other individuals had been excommunicated for various sins, but rarely did a family of our commitment and standing in the church arrive at such an impasse. In most cases, when there were differences, there were avenues of resolution by which problems could be aired, solutions found, and confidence restored. We spent much time retracing our steps, trying to find clues which would enlighten us in the position in which we found ourselves. Were we simply arrogant and self-centered, determined to choose, as we were told, "an easier way?" Or had we reached a point where our desire for honesty demanded that we face up to what we saw as an inconsistent interpretation of Scripture.

My husband and I remembered certain incidents that had caused us to question practices and teachings of the church. In earlier years we had simply accepted the notion that the "The One True Visible Church" could not be in error in any sense. But as a young couple still in our twenties, we had attended a general conference of our denomination that had unsettled us a bit. Here we saw respected leaders in the church, qualified ministers in whom we placed great confidence, take opposing sides on issues, presenting their views with such integrity and vehemence that both sides seemed right. Yet, only one side could win, and we weren't sure it was always the right side that did. Naively, we had assumed that church policies were generated in total harmony since surely they were made in heaven and handed down as though symbolically written in stone. Yet, such experiences, though not fully understood, had not demanded we make any drastic changes in our lives. Was there some hidden fault within us which reached back into what psychologists believe is the seedbed of adult life, our childhood? How could the warm, loving simplicity of a Holdeman Mennonite childhood produce a dissident in later years?

A PRIVILEGED CHILDHOOD

Chapter Two

A song my mother used to sing began with the words, "How dear to my heart are the scenes of my childhood, when fond recollection has brought them to view." Sadly, many people are not blest with memories of a happy childhood. Some are, of course, or at least they recall occasions when happy events occurred, but for too many, childhood was a traumatic event, leaving them with lifelong scars. However, the Holdeman Mennonite home in which I grew up was a loving home with parents who loved their children without reservation, enough to care for them and all of their physical and emotional needs. It was also important to them to teach us about Jesus from little on up. I imagine I learned the familiar song, "Jesus loves me this I know, for the Bible tells me so" when I still sat on my mother's lap. She loved to sing, and very early I learned the words and melody of the wonderful hymns of the church. I still sing them to this day.

Even though I took my parents' love and devotion for granted, many years later I would learn just how privileged I was. In my late forties I had the opportunity to finally become a college student. During the first semester of my return to college, I took a class called "Re-entry for Women." This class was made up of women, most of whom were mature students who were endeavoring to deal with the hurts of their past as they made new lives for themselves. As the class progressed and the women were given opportunity to expose the pain of the past within a supportive environment, I was appalled. Nearly every student had gone through terrible experiences in their childhoods, from alcoholic parents to child molestation. Divorce was nearly universal among their parents, and many spoke of being uprooted and moved from place to place. They had already dealt with so much anger and pain. Many of them struggled with depression.

When it was my turn to present my story, I was nearly embarrassed. It seemed unfair that I had experienced so much security and genuine happiness as a child. I have discovered, however, a truth which has reaffirmed something I suspected even while I was growing up. I say it to myself occasionally because it provides positive reinforcement to my inner thought life, although there is no credit I myself can claim; I have simply been blest. And it is this: I am one of the happiest people I know. It goes without saying that I am not happy every moment, and that I have gone through sorrow and pain, particularly with the early death of my mother and with other challenges in my life. But that inner security which was given me by loving Christian parents is always a foundation that supports me, even in less pleasant times. And my view of Jesus as a friend who loves me without reservation and is with me constantly gives me a security and a confidence that together, He and I can survive any challenge. I do not feel abandoned and alone, nor beaten down by overwhelming cares of life. My trust is deeply rooted.

What are the ingredients of a happy childhood? Many things, I presume, but having loving parents surely is the foundation. My mother had grown up in a home where there had been a certain amount of conflict, and it was her firm determination that her own home would be different. Having married a good and kind man, not to mention handsome, she proceeded, with his loving support, to create the home of her dreams. The fact that they had no money had little importance. After all, he had a steady job with a decent income, and after a few months of marriage, a small house was provided along with the job. Her parents generously gave them a milk cow as a wedding gift, and with the purchase of a used wooden table and four chairs plus a used bed frame, they set up housekeeping. It was still in the days before the arrival of modern appliances, and refrigerators were unknown, at least in the country. Instead, an ice box served as cold storage for milk and butter. This was a small wooden box attached to a north window and covered with a gunny sack which was dampened with water several times a day. The breeze blowing through the wet sack cooled the fresh milk and home-churned butter within. There was no need to keep perishables for a long time—you used them up or gave away each day's excess because there would be fresh milk, etc. tomorrow. However, by the time I arrived, my parents had a "real ice box," which was a box covered with white granite coating with shelves in it, and at the top, a compartment in which to place a chunk of ice, which the "ice man" brought periodically. I'm sure my mother felt thankful to have such an advanced convenience to make food storage easier.

By the time we children came along, my parents had moved to "the big house" on the large vineyard ranch four miles west of our small town of Livingston. It wasn't large, but had a nice living room/dining room combination which made it seem spacious. It included two bedrooms and an enclosed sun porch, which became my older brother's bedroom. It was one of only two houses on the property that had indoor plumbing, so we children never had the "out house" experience, except when we visited relatives. None of my relatives had indoor plumbing when I was a child, and staying overnight in their homes was always fun. Who would have known that last, after-dark trip to the outhouse could be such an adventure! We would take a flashlight, shining the light all around, and then race to our place of business where we would hear, or pretend to hear, scary noises, which would then send us flying back to the house, full of shrieks and giggles. I can remember taking a Saturday night bath in a large round tub placed in the kitchen, but I can't remember whether only my cousin and I bathed in the water or if more family members would use the same offering. I think it depended on how dirty the water was judged to be after someone before you had bathed. It was quite a privilege to be first.

My dad was the grandson of immigrants, but the man he worked for was himself an immigrant from the old country. In true American style, he had come to this country nearly penniless and had worked hard for the fifty cents a day he was paid, half of which he had saved. Now his son owned the largest ranch in our community and my father was his foreman. Untrained, and with an education that went only through the fourth grade, Dad was nevertheless quick to pick up the skills needed to manage the many acres of Thompson seedless grapes grown on the Arakelian Ranch. In the summer the long rows of grapes were picked into boxes, brought to the main ranch area by wagons pulled by a team of horses, and processed for raisins in the dehydrator also on the property. My Dad's cheerful, kind attitude made him a pleasant boss to work for, and the day laborers responded to his kindness by being hard-working and dependable. He would work in this position for about twenty years before moving on to his own ranch only a mile down the same road we'd traveled so many years.

We children were young during the Great Depression of the 1930's, but our family never suffered from its stresses. We were secure in our large, comfortable frame house provided by Dad's job, with a steady income sufficient to meet our simple needs. My dad, however, with his tender heart, found himself in a most difficult position. During these difficult years, men needing a job would arrive almost daily at the ranch in search of work, any work, just to buy a few groceries for their hungry families. There were simply not enough jobs to be had, and even during harvest there were more applicants than positions. Finally my dad and his boss worked out a system which eased their troubled hearts a bit. Each desperate man would receive at least one day's work and one day's pay, enough to buy a few groceries for his family. While they didn't have a job to offer everyone, neither my dad nor his boss, Mr. Arakelian, could bear to send anyone away empty-handed. I also know that there were times when some of those dollars came out of the pocket money of my soft-hearted father and his desire to be generous. He had known poverty as a child, and he carried those memories with him, even as he thanked God continuously for His provision in his adult life.

ACHIEVING THE DREAM OF OWNERSHIP

Chapter Three

During these years when Dad was foreman on the ranch, my parents were frugal and cautious, and the money in their bank account began to build until they started to think about buying their own farm. As I remember Dad saying, he was paid $100 a month, half of which they put away in a savings account. Then, when I was six my parents bought their own ranch about one mile from the home place where we lived. Situated near the Merced River, it was a dream come true for my parents and would become a sort of country paradise for our family. The farm was planted in almonds with a grape vineyard at the front of the property near the road, and some open land below the house. This would later be seeded into grazing pastures for the small herd of dairy cows Dad purchased. Since my grandfather had never owned "a shovelful of dirt," as my father phrased it, my dad's ability to buy his own farm, even though it was a relatively small ranch of thirty-two acres, was a real step forward. He was now "a land owner," with income property, a very meaningful position during the Depression. However, it would be at least a year before the family would move off of the large ranch to the new home site.

The farm my parents bought had only a small, very old wood-frame house, so the first improvement needed was to build a new home. My mother wasn't particular about many things, but she did want a large kitchen and pantry, as well as a cellar to hold the rows and rows of canned fruits and vegetables she put up every summer. Dad hired a carpenter, whose family lived in the small house during the construction of the new house, using the water tank house as additional sleeping quarters for their sons.

After the new house was built, with two bedrooms downstairs and three upstairs, it was known by our extended family as "Anna's big house," although it was not large by today's standards. Along with the generous kitchen and its separate pantry, it had a good-sized dinning room, an average size living room, and five bedrooms. However, it was the indoor bathroom that impressed many of our relatives. The tub was built-in on one side of the room, that is, it was not the old style that stood on its own four legs, but instead fit snugly against the wall. There was no shower over the tub at first; that would come later. In those days, one bathroom was considered adequate, no matter how large the family, so of course, there was not a second bath upstairs. Instead, we still had the traditional outhouse near the shed, which was convenient for the male members of the family as they worked out on the farm.

Our family moved in before the upstairs was completed, so mother used the "spare" bedroom downstairs, which would later become the guest room, to place the double bed the boys slept in as well as the single bed which was mine. Both of our beds, and in fact, much of our furniture came from used furniture stores; my parents had simple tastes and elegant furniture was not a priority, nor, for that matter, would it have been acceptable in the religious culture in which I was raised. However, the gas stove and electric refrigerator in the kitchen were purchased new and were quite impressive. The days of the old ice box were definitely over, and my mother enjoyed some of the recent conveniences that were available, including an electric mixer on a stand, which was a new item touted as "making all your cooking projects easier."

We children were not dismayed at not having our own rooms, particularly since we knew they would be finished soon. It would be almost a year before they were completed and we children moved upstairs, the boys sharing a room facing the north, and mine being the south room. My room had two very nice windows looking out over the front porch and a portion of the driveway. There was a third bedroom with windows looking toward the west which was the guest room, and with the many visitors my parents continually invited, either for one night or for a few weeks, it was occupied frequently. The downstairs guest bedroom would become home to my mother's father after the death of her mother, and later to my dad's mother after the death of his father. My parents did not hesitate to provide care for elderly parents, even while living busy lives and raising their own children.

As it turned out when we first moved into the new house, sharing a bedroom proved to be delightful, making bedtime a special treat since our mom read to us nightly. We were, in fact, eager to go to bed when evening came because of our enthusiasm for the stories she read. Bedtime reading became the highlight of our day, and Mother's obvious pleasure in catching up on books she had not had the opportunity to read earlier made this a time we looked forward to. I wonder if anyone still reads the books we enjoyed back then? Mom read to us all of the Five Little Peppers series, as well as Louisa May Alcott's books, particularly Little Women and Little Men. Also on the list were The Poor Little Rich Girl, Daddy Long Legs, and many other delightful books which extended our world past our own small farm. In between the popular children's books she would read Bible stories written for children, even reading what must have been challenging for us, the classic Pilgrim's Progress. I still remember how exciting it was to begin a new story. The purchase of a new book, with its colorful jacket cover usually depicting the book's characters or some scene within the story, was carefully studied before the book was opened and the reading began. There was a sense of wonder and speculation as Mom began to read, and we knew that we would travel to lands and experiences new to us as the story progressed from evening to evening. What a wonderful way to expose children to the joy of reading!

But of all the privileges of my childhood, growing up along the river was one of the best. There is something about a river that has always intrigued the romantic spirit of man, and writers such as Mark Twain and others have used that fascination to advantage. A river has significance far beyond the mere flow of water, and certainly we children were enchanted by its invitation to experience and explore. In summer, our greatest delight was to refresh ourselves within its cool waters as we spent hours swimming in the Merced River flowing about an eighth of a mile north of our house. The river bed right below our house was a stretch that was wide between the two banks and therefore shallow and non-threatening. Since it was only about knee-high, it was ideal for the splashing and playing young children like to do as they cool off on a hot summer day. We knew there was deeper water upstream where the river made a sharp bend, but if we stayed in the shallows, Mom was confident we'd be fine.

The river banks were covered with giant oak trees, interspersed with other native trees and with shrubs and vines of every description, creating a cool and mysterious place to explore. There were trails that led through this area we called a jungle, possibly made by horses that occasionally came as far upstream as our swimming area. In the spring, the beauty of fresh green leaves and blossoming bushes along with the scent of these blooms turned the entire landscape into a sort of wonderland.

For the first summer or two, Mom would always escort us and stay to watch us swim in the river. As we got older, Mother was more relaxed about letting us go on our own down to the river to swim, and she trusted us to stay away from adventures into the deep and unknown areas. However, like most children, we never told her everything. Had she known about the time we decided to follow the river downstream and around the bend, just the three of us going further than we had ever ventured before, she would have withdrawn our privileges. But even on that one particular occasion when we decided to "explore" and were caught for a time in a current stronger than we expected, we did manage to survive. My older brother had developed a strong sense of responsibility for his younger siblings, and while our lives were in his hands during that particular expedition, he managed to get us back to safety again. Fortunately, that experience taught us to respect the force of the river, and we never took those same chances again. As we sat on the bank after pulling ourselves up a steep bank, my brother suggested, "Let's not tell Mom, okay?"

I am not sure if my childhood was really as idyllic as I remember, but I do know that all the ingredients were there: Two loving parents who loved each other and loved and enjoyed us kids and had the means to care for us without undo financial stress. We were taught early on about Jesus' love for us, and Bible reading was a regular part of our lives. Our dad was firmly convinced that other than extreme illness or death there was no good reason to miss church, and we certainly didn't. I can remember having a severe cold and being allowed to stay in the back seat of the car during the service, with blankets, water, snacks, and a good book. We didn't stay home for the common cold!

Also, church was not a hardship for us, but a place we loved to go. I had inherited my mother's love of singing, and from early childhood I sang lustily and memorized the words of those wonderful old hymns. On Sunday mornings we children looked forward to our Sunday School classes, and I especially enjoyed those times when my mom was the teacher. She was gifted in her ability to teach and knew how to make it fun to be in class. Her love of teaching was another attribute she passed on to me. Many years later I would have the opportunity she never had, to go to college and prepare to be a teacher in both the public schools and later, a private Christian school. Many things would transpire before that opportunity would come to pass.

SCHOOL DAYS

Chapter Four

I loved school from the start. I entered the first grade in the little four-room wood-framed school which housed the primary grades in Livingston, my home town, about two months shy of my sixth birthday. My mother recalled that she had let me go with my big brother, Jim, to "visit school" when I was only three and a half, a wonderful experience which stuck in my memory. Jim was so proud of his little sister that he took her to school to show her off, apparently without worrying about who would take her to the bathroom or what he would do if she cried. Somehow it all worked out fine. A few years later it would be time for me to begin my own wonderful experience called "going to school," a place I always loved and where I was able to excel.

My first teacher, Mrs. Sheesley, was considered "strict," but I learned early to love and to please her. While she was sparing with praise, I was a quick learner, and a child knows intuitively whether or not she is behaving in an approved manner. My parents had taught all of us children well, and we followed the rules carefully. I learned to read in the first grade, and I suppose I brought little books home to read to my mom. However, I do remember showing my parents I could read the newspaper, skipping the hard words, I suspect, but it was a feat I was quite proud of.

The second year in school coincided with the beginning of World War II, and since we had no radio, I knew little about what was going on. I did know, however, that one of my good friends, a boy of Japanese decent, was suddenly missing from our classroom. I later learned there was much anti-Japanese feeling, even in our little town where Japanese families were successful farmers and model citizens, but my parents were Christians and took the Biblical injunction to love everyone seriously. Because they believed it, I also learned that "Jesus loves everyone, no matter what color, race or creed," and that everyone deserved respect and acceptance. In our family we were not afflicted with racial discrimination, for which I am so appreciative.

Of course, as I grew older, I also learned that there were differences in the way I was brought up and that of my little friends. For example, in about the third grade some of my friends would began to talk about radio shows they listened to and even movies they attended, talking about "movie stars" and entertainment that I had no knowledge of. Since this was not a part of my world, I'm sure I asked questions but do not remember feeling dismayed. Even though my parents were not harsh in their judgments, we were taught that radios and movies were "worldly," and therefore not a part of our lifestyle as Holdeman Mennonite believers. Television, of course, had not yet arrived and would have been spurned by my parents anyway. However, I listened to my friends tell about radio characters such as The Lone Ranger and movie stars popular in the '40's, and wondered if I was really missing out on something important. Occasionally I would tell my close friends about the books my mom was reading to us and some of the characters in these stories. Generally, the differences between my lifestyle and that of my school-mates seemed minor and did not make me feel deprived.

As I continued through school, it seemed I was always blessed with wonderful teachers, each of which contributed to my education in some special way. For example, my fourth grade teacher read the wonderful book, <u>The Secret Garden</u>, which became my favorite children's book of all time. She read with a Yorkshire accent, which made the story come alive. This was also the year when, during the yearly revivals held at our church, I first stood to show my decision to make my faith personal and to ask Jesus into my heart. I was a bit young, being only nine years old, while eleven and twelve were considered a more acceptable age for children to "come to the years of accountability." Still, this is when I felt the calling of the Lord and I responded. I suspect that due to my mother's teaching I was more knowledgeable about Jesus and His great love for us than some may have been at that age. After all, I had literally gown up on the church bench, having been born into a family to whom church attendance was essential. I'd heard the Gospel all my life through hearing the Bible read for morning family devotions and by listening to Bible story books my mother read, not to mention the many, many sermons I was exposed to sitting at my mother's side in church. Also, Sunday School was very important to me as a child, and in each of our individual classes the Bible was taught at a level children could understand.

My fifth grade teacher loved music, and our music period every day was my favorite time. She even let me play her auto harp, which I picked up on quickly. By this time I was already singing harmony with my mother on the way to and from church, so it was simple for me to transpose that talent to playing the auto harp. I often wondered what it would be like to play the piano, but I had already learned that musical instruments of any kind were unacceptable in the church we were a part of. I suspect I didn't beg my parents for something that I knew was so totally off limits.

It was my sixth grade teacher who loved and shared poetry as part of her daily lesson plan that impacted my life strongly. She would have us get our lunch boxes and coats from the closet, and on the board she would write two to four lines of poetry from whatever poem we were memorizing. In the last ten minutes of the class, we would repeat what we had already learned and then learn the new lines on the board. By this method she would help us memorize about twenty poems during the school year, many of them very long. What a gift she gave me, and how I would like to tell her that years later I would write my own poetry, and that because of her thoughtfulness, I would find joy in expressing myself in such a way.

Both seventh and eighth grade teachers were also greatly appreciated. In the seventh grade, I again had a musical teacher who asked me and two of my Holdeman friends to sing "harmony" in a little Christmas program she put together for the season. Since our Holdeman Mennonite culture did not allow musical instruments, many of us learned to sing beautiful four-part harmony in our churches, a wonderful way to sing songs of worship. This would carry over into singing at home also and was a favorite activity when guests were invited. Our school teacher also encouraged artistic talent, and I remember one of the students was a wonderful artist who did a painting of the manger in Bethlehem complete with the Baby Jesus. It was done on butcher paper, but it covered our entire back wall above the lockers. References to the Christian faith were commonplace when I was in school in the 1940's, and there were no repercussions. In fact, one of the teachers while I was in my elementary years, actually began her class with devotions—a few Scripture verses and a prayer. Most students went to church, and generally speaking, we were either Protestant or Catholic. I didn't know anyone who didn't go to church at all.

During my eighth grade year, our classroom was right next to the principal's office, and these were the years when corporal punishment was still common practice. We would listen for how many swats it would take before the disobedient child would began to wail loudly; usually it would take three or four. I would cringe, sitting in my desk in the adjacent room, and inwardly thank God that my parents did not believe in spanking. Their form of discipline was usually verbal—reminding us that being obedient to parents was the same as being obedient to God and something we all would want to do. My mom did on occasion, however, sit me down in a chair in the middle of the kitchen and require me to sit there until I had an "attitude adjustment."

When the school year ended and it was time to graduate, I was one of two speakers selected to speak at the graduation. My talk was a simple review of our school years to this point—starting in the small, wooden school building that housed first and second grade, then moving to "the big school" for the remainder of our elementary school years. For some reason, I wanted very badly to have a white graduation dress. Perhaps this was the preferred color, or maybe I just wanted it to be a very special occasion. Little Holdeman Mennonite girls did not wear white dresses, but to my surprise, my mom bought a length of cloth of a white, linen-type fabric, which, I learned, she planned to dye blue after the big event. Buying white material and sewing a white dress was a little risky for her since she, as a deacon's wife, was definitely stepping over the line. However, I was ecstatic. Along with the lovely white dress she sewed for me, I was privileged to have my first corsage, a lovely, sweet-smelling gardenia. Furthermore, the graduation was held in the new Court Theater downtown, a place I never would have had entrance to since movies were off limits. The uniqueness of the place made it very special.

By the time I was in eighth grade I had experienced occasionally what it meant to be a member of an ultra-conservative church. There was a period of several months while in the sixth grade when a girlfriend and I wore long, cotton stockings, even in the heat of summer. Whether we did it to appear "righteous" to other people, or if we thought it would please God, I no longer remember. But the funny thing was that without discussing it with each other, we both came to school one summer morning without them. As we looked at each other, we laughed and laughed. I guess our efforts at "holiness" had tested our endurance and abruptly ended.

There were also a few times when I'd been invited to birthday parties at classmates' homes and wasn't allowed to go. The idea here was that we were "set apart" from those who were not members of our church—that we could have them as friends, but not as associates. Unlike my non-Holdeman friends, I always wore my hair in braids, and my mother sewed most of my dresses. However, she was a good seamstress, and my dresses were not so different than my friends, although they were not made "fancy" with lace and trimmings as the "store bought" clothes of the other girls. There were some students whose parents were economically stressed and unable to dress their daughters as well as others, so I was not the only one whose clothes were a bit "different." I knew this difference stemmed from the fact that I was a member of the "one true church," while other classmates were Baptist or Methodist or Catholic, considered by our church as "worldly churches." Occasionally we would have discussions as classmates in which we compared church practices, but these were not in-depth discussions. I think we Holdeman students concluded that our friends would not understand our church's teachings, particularly as they applied to how we dressed and what we were or were not allowed to do.

My Teenage Years

Chapter Five

By the time I reached high school, I had learned to live in two worlds—my school world and my church world. I truly loved both, and knew how to conduct myself in such a way that they did not conflict. My church world crossed over into my school days with a few rules that I was expected to follow, which were not difficult. My hair could not be curled or allowed to hang straight but needed to be braided, with one braid on each side of my head, then crossed over on top and held with bobby pins. This would include a little wave in front of the braid, which softened the look a bit, but there was no variance in how I did my hair, day in and day out. To "let my hair down" would have been paramount to rebellion in my church, and I certainly didn't want that.

My dress-styles were not totally different from those of the other girls since nearly all girls wore dresses, even during my high school years. My mother was apparently more lenient than some mothers because I was allowed to wear skirts and blouses now and then which very few Holdeman girls did. Nearly all of my clothes were home-sewn, although a few "ready-made" outfits were bought at Penny's or similar stores, if they were judged to be "plain" enough. So I didn't feel like a total odd-ball, although I was easily identified as a Mennonite girl. It was popular then to wear tennis shoes with no socks, or loafers with socks rolled down, and I was no longer wearing the long, brown stockings I'd worn in the sixth grade. I don't remember anyone wearing sandals, but when they did become popular, Holdeman girls were not allowed to wear them.

Aside from clothes, there was also the issue of involvement. One of the things high school students enjoy so much is the social and sporting events that occur while attending school. There was Friday night football, which later in the year would become basketball or baseball. Then there were the school dances, the school plays and musical performances that it seemed like everyone except me could attend. That wasn't true, of course. Many years later I discovered that there were other girls raised in strict homes, several of whom came from Catholic families and also had many restrictions on their social lives. Very few kids had cars in those days; I think only a few seniors were so lucky. Therefore, parents simply could refuse to provide transportation or not allow teen friends to pick up their kids, and they effectively kept them at home. I did hear a few stories of girls sneaking out of basement windows, but that was likely rare.

However, I gathered a lot of positive reinforcement from doing well in the academics of my various classes, and since I usually earned "A's" I did gain some recognition. My grades made it possible to be in the California Scholarship Federation, the club that promoted academic excellence, but it was something I kept quiet about in my church circles. Any "club" was suspect, even if it met during the school day rather than in the evening. I wasn't highly gifted athletically, and our high school only did intramural sports for girls, which meant our teams didn't travel to compete with other schools. Their competition was entirely between the various periods of PE classes. I did love to run track, but again, it was within our own physical education class.

Our PE classes caused some concern, however. Girls were expected to wear white shorts and a blouse, but shorts were off limits to Holdeman students. I remember when I began as a freshman, my mother let me buy a pair of slightly longer blue shorts, but when revival meetings came around, these items of clothing had to be discarded in favor of blue "peddle pushers," as they were called. These were pants that came to the mid-calf. There was one Pentecostal girl who could not wear pants of any kind and wore a skirt and blouse instead. I looked at her with admiration but was glad to be able to wear "pants" for P.E. Very likely, wearing such clothing was not approved, but if no one made a fuss we were able to get by.

THE TRAUMA OF
LEAVING SCHOOL

Chapter Six

At the beginning of my third year of high school, our church held its annual revivals, and that year we had invited two ministers from Kansas, a state where students were required to stop their schooling after completing the eighth grade only. High school was not even an option. These ministers came to our congregation of Livingston with the firm belief that anything higher than eighth grade led to pride, and therefore, all students should consider their education as finished at that level. However, California had a different law; every student had to be in school until age sixteen, after which continued education was optional. I began to see where this philosophy was headed, and, in fact, I saw the writing on the wall. Sure enough, the pressure was on as my sixteenth birthday was coming up in November of my junior year.

Looking back, I wonder why I was so submissive. It wasn't my parents who pushed me to quit—it was my strong desire to be faithful to my church, whose decisions I believed represented God's plan for my life. It also helped that several of my friends were also making this move to drop out that same year. They seemed to be happy to be out from under the burden of homework and daily classes, but I was giving up the thing I loved more than anything—the opportunity to learn and the interaction with teachers I admired. However, I wanted to follow the teachings of my church which believed that "higher education" led to nothing more than prideful arrogance, the sin most hated by God.

I will never forget the day I dropped out. As I took my drop out slip to every teacher to sign, they looked up at me with surprise and said, "Why, Leona . . ." and I would begin to cry all over again. I cried throughout the day but I did what I believed was the right thing to do. My own feelings were not valued compared to "doing the right thing."

In addition to dropping out of high school, we were reminded that photographs of any kind were forbidden, and I had purchased the yearbook or annual in both my freshman and sophomore years. In my sincere effort to "conform," I decided these books I treasured would have to go. I remember how I struggled, how I prayed, to have the grace to throw these books into our wood burning stove, but one day I decided I would struggle no more. I would just be obedient. Unfortunately, my mother had given me her yearbook from her freshman year, and I decided that would have to be sacrificed also. Looking back, it does seem that the fact she'd had it all these years and that I, her daughter, should make the decision to burn it, was nothing short of ridiculous. However, when one uses legalistic measures in an effort to please God, rational thinking doesn't enter into the decision-making process. I must have felt some satisfaction that I had been obedient to the mandates of the church. Today I so regret this action. How I would love to have that yearbook as a memory of my mom in her youth. Since photos were forbidden, taking pictures and then preserving them as keepsakes was one of life's pleasures of which we denied ourselves. This requirement was based on the second of the Ten Commandments that states we are not to make for ourselves "graven images, nor are we to worship them." One could certainly argue that making idols and then falling down to worshiping them is a far cry from keeping a photograph that documents a memorable moment in one's life, but who was I to take a stand against church doctrine!

Now, without the structure of school life, it became problematic as to how I should spend my time. Fortunately, the opportunity to become a mother's helper soon arose as there were a series of young mothers who needed help after the birth of their new babies. This was a happy option for me since I loved babies, and in our household we'd had a shortage of them. To live in the home of a family with a new baby, to help with simple housework and care for the children in the home, and to rock to sleep or diaper or even bathe the new baby was delightful. I fixed my enthusiasm on my new experiences as a caregiver.

Yes, I missed school terribly, but if I could be a mother's helper in taking care of precious little newborns, surely that was second best. I had three or four such opportunities, as well as being a helper to two aunts I loved who had small children. I remember cooking French toast for one aunt's family who was quite taken aback with my efforts.

My mother had made the batter salty, while my aunt's family was used to it being quite sweet, so after one taste, no one wanted to eat my offerings. Fortunately, my uncle proclaimed that my cooking "wouldn't kill them," and they should eat what I fixed and not waste it. Both these aunts were marvelous cooks, so I decided my talents were probably better used in caring for the young children of the family.

As the summer came to a close and the new school year was about to commence, I received a phone call from my high school counselor. He wondered how I was doing and would I have time to come in and help with some filing, etc? I was so lonesome for school I would have come in to do janitorial work if someone had asked, so of course I said I would. Once there he asked me, "Is there any way you could come back to school?" I said I thought that might be possible, and I would ask my parents. After all, they were not the ones who had encouraged me to drop out. Sure enough, they had observed my restlessness and my lack of purpose and they quickly gave me permission to return. By this time I was driving, and I was allowed to drive to school most days, although I occasionally rode the school bus. I wasn't too concerned about how to get there so long as I could once again be in that learning environment I so enjoyed. I was back in my element, and it seemed there was would be no disciplinary action by the church because of my return. At school I was expected to pull together more units than one normally gathers in a year since I had missed most of my junior year, but I was willing to work hard in the hopes that I could graduate with my class.

My counselor planned with me how to accumulate the units I would need to graduate. I would be able to make up some work in one class, gain a few credits by working in the library at lunch, and take a correspondence class from the state university on the side. I also signed up for a "public speaking" class taught by my counselor, which would count at English IV, the fourth year of English required by my high school to graduate. I was shy and had no idea how I would accomplish the art of public speaking. This training would be the coursework taught by our instructor in order for students to achieve the confidence to speak publicly. And did I even question where I would ever speak "publicly?" Women did not speak publicly in my culture.

We started simply by doing pantomime, acting out a simple story for our class on the small stage in the classroom. Later, we would select a scene from a favorite novel, memorize it and then dramatize it for our class. Later, we moved to the area of debate. I had never done this, nor had my partner, a girlfriend I had gone to school with since grade school. We did our research, wrote our thesis, and began writing our arguments. We needed to consider both sides of the argument chosen as the topic that year, both pro and con, because we were in fact preparing for a debate tournament to be held at a high school in San Francisco, a two hour drive from home. We were all inexperienced, products of a small-town high school, and our advisor kept reminding us that we weren't going to beat the competition, but were going simply to "gain some experience."

However, things turned out rather unexpectedly! With what seemed like unusual luck, my partner and I often managed to draw the side of the argument we were most passionate about, and therefore won many of the preliminary rounds. Eventually we reached the finals, and again we found ourselves assigned to the side of the argument for which we were better prepared. We were dumbfounded when we took first place in the tournament in the category of debate. We could hardly imagine how that had happened. We went home on the bus in a state of exhilaration, holding our trophies and wondering how two inexperienced, small-town girls had managed to take first place in the tournament.

We were able to participate in one more tournament, which we also won, before the ministers of our local church came to visit my parents. Since my father was an ordained deacon in the church, we were expected to set an example, but this was not the example they had in mind. Their words were stern and to the point: Either I gave up this nonsense of participating on a high school debate team or steps would be taken to reel me in, as well as my parents, to walking the spiritual line that was expected. I had known that participating in forensics wasn't exactly Holdeman behavior, so when the reporter came from our hometown paper, I made sure that my picture was not taken. Our church did not believe in having one's "likeness" taken, so I politely refused, and only my partner's photograph was published. However, the story was written up, and my name was there in black and white. This was publicity of which my church did not approve, and, as I would learn, would not tolerate.

I was disappointed, of course, and telling my debate partner that I could no longer participate was especially difficult. I encouraged her to find a new partner, but she wasn't interested. She didn't think she would find another student with whom she could develop the close rapport she and I had, so for both of us, our competitive debate days were over. I had made a choice between continuing something I had learned to love, and was apparently good at, for harmony with my church. This was by far the most important choice for me, and the fact that it kept my parents from getting in trouble was a significant factor. Besides, I had plenty of homework as I tried to do nearly two years of high school in one year. Being a teenager, I did sometimes procrastinate and almost didn't finish in time. In fact, I completed my correspondence course providing enough credits to graduate with only a matter of days, maybe hours, to spare. I was grateful to squeak by just in time to be able to share this special occasion with my school friends.

I was one of four or five graduation speakers, and my topic was "The Way to Peace through Morals and Ideals." I had achieved an important goal, that of being able to graduate from high school with my peers. My counselor tried to encourage me to apply to a Mennonite College in Kansas, but I informed him that "our Mennonites" didn't believe those "other Mennonites" were even Christians.

Besides graduation, I had another very important interest: the young man who was courting me, secretly of course, had asked for my hand in marriage! Because of the current war going on, the Korean conflict, being married would help him get the classification he needed as a conscientious objector. I was at loose ends since I'd finished my education and there was no college career in my future, so it seemed like the right thing to do. I was seventeen, nearly eighteen, by the time our wedding day in October of 1952 would arrive. My dream, as with every young girl, was to marry and have a family of my own. It was time to plan this most important event, my wedding.

The Other Side of the Story (Willis's Life)

Chapter Seven

Even though I had been raised in a frugal lifestyle, the truth was my father had a very good job, and both parents were loving, caring individuals who brought us up in a very supportive way. Naturally, I assumed that all families were like mine—we all looked the same when we came to church Sunday mornings. Before long I would learn this was a misconception, and that even in our very conservative church, there was deprivation and dysfunction hidden within a number of families.

I discovered this after our wedding as I began to get acquainted with my new husband. Since courtship was frowned on, even prohibited, in our church, couples were not given permission to spend time alone together. They were to find their mates through prayer and God's guidance only, which meant that the majority of couples knew little about the mate they planned to marry. This was certainly true of my husband and me. The difference in our up-bringing was quite pronounced. We went to the same church, but we did not have the same kind of homes. The fact that my husband's mother had died when he was two was an incredible loss for him and his siblings. Also contributing to the stress in the family was the depression of the 1930's and the fact that they lived right in the path of the constantly blowing winds, a phenomena of nature called "The Dust Bowl," against which there were no defenses. Resulting in part by the over-cultivating of farm land, Kansas farmers were in the middle of it all as the winds blew, taking the top soil with it. Western Kansas was hard hit, and the Nichols family was located right in its path and would be one of many families who lost their farm and had to move in order to survive.

I knew my husband came from a large family and that he had lost his mother and had been raised by a stepmother, but I didn't have an inkling of how difficult his life had been. His parents did their best, but there were so many strikes against them. Extreme poverty and family size contributed to their challenges, and no matter how hard they worked, there was never enough money to live comfortably. In Willis's family of birth, there were eight living children, he being number seven. In his step-mom's family there were three children when she became a widow, so at her marriage to Dad they became a family of thirteen. A year after the marriage, the third set of children began to arrive, and soon there would be three more girls and a son, bringing the total to fifteen children plus two parents. What parents could possibly care for so many, especially during The Great Depression, a very difficult time all over this country. Even much smaller families struggled to put food on the table.

The drought coupled with hot, dusty winds swept across the prairies, not only destroying all vegetation in its path, but infiltrating even the best-built houses through cracks and windows until it was possible to literally shovel out the accumulated dirt. Occasionally, clean clothes hanging on the line became too dirty to be brought in and would have to be rewashed. Hard-working farmers would plant crops only to have the seedlings blown out, or if they did take root, there would be no rain to provide the moisture needed for growth.

I can imagine the desperation Willis's parents must have felt as they tried again and again to grow a crop, only to have it lost to the ever-blowing wind. Dad and the older brothers did their best to find other work, but jobs were scarce. One brother was "farmed out" to a family for work in another community, a blessing because it was one less mouth to feed, and even though his wages were meager, he was expected to send a few dollars home as often as possible. As the older girls became capable of the hard work expected of women in those days, they did what they could to help ease Mom's heavy load. One or two found work as housemaids for some of the more fortunate people in the community. Wages were low, but again, it would be one less mouth to feed and it brought in a few dollars for the family at home.

As the stress of the "Dirty Thirties" continued, providing for the family became ever more difficult. Dad and Mom eventually came to the decision they would have to pack up and move out of Western Kansas, abandoning their farm. What a difficult decision that must have been! The property went into foreclosure, but whether they had a farm sale of machinery and equipment or simply left things behind or gave them away, Willis isn't sure. When they left Fredonia, Kansas for California several years later, he does remember a farm sale at that location.

Willis was young, about seven years old, when they lost their place, and I'm sure the atmosphere in the home was one of worry and concern. Other than having very limited food on the table at all the meals, the children were likely not aware of the desperation of these times, particularly since other families in the area were going through the same thing. It was Mom and Dad who carried the heavy weight of responsibility for their large family, and as with most large families, the children were not included in decision-making. When it came time to move, Dad loaded up some of their farm equipment to take with them to Fredonia, a small town in Eastern Kansas that had escaped the fierce winds. Just packing up their family and basic household goods would in itself be a taxing experience, and walking away from their own farm was heart-wrenching. Willis's dad never got over the pain of losing their farm, and would get tears in his eyes whenever he talked about it years later.

It's hard to believe Mom and Dad Nichols and the ten youngest children managed to fit in the family car and make the trip to Fredonia. The five eldest children had already left home and had either married or were working at jobs away from home. Leaving behind friends, family, and home is never easy, but Mom and Dad did what parents have undertaken since the beginning of time—doing what had to be done.

When they arrived in Fredonia the congregation welcomed them. Willis's dad was a minister, and his position in the church made their family a pleasant addition to the small congregation. Soon they found a house to rent that was sufficient in size for their large family, especially since children were expected to double-up in bedroom space. Now, instead of having their own home, they lived on a rented farm with a house that was a bit small, but at least the dust didn't blow here. Willis has some happy memories of living in the Fredonia area, particularly one home with a large wooded area just across the road that they could explore and enjoy, a wonderful place to play in their free time. One advantage of a large family was that there were always siblings near their own ages who could be playmates. Of course, there were also the constant farm chores, both morning and evening, taking care of the chickens, cows, and horses that every farm family maintained. Having older brothers, Willis doesn't remember much field work that he was involved in; rather, helping by hoeing or watering the vegetable garden, essential for survival, was a task that frequently fell to him.

Things didn't go as well as they hoped in Eastern Kansas. Dad was quite enterprising, successfully raising turkeys for market for a couple of years, but this was followed by a bad year in which he ended up losing everything. Mom was ingenious in her efforts to put food on the table with little or no food supplies. Her homemade bread was second to none, and her "milk soup" made with milk and dough gave the family something hot to go with the tasty bread. Milk soup was made with seasoned milk and a dough made of flour, salt, a little water, and rubbed between the palms of the hands to let small pieces of dough drop into the milk. This also thickened it a bit. For variety there were potato patties, grated potatoes held together with egg and flour and fried in the lard they had rendered from the last hog butchering. These were considered very tasty, and my husband remembers this as something he appreciated, although at times the servings were limited since the family was so large.

During this difficult time, one of the older girls hired out to be a "mother's helper" to a wealthy family, who had taken her with them to the far-away land of California. She had come home with stories to tell: California was a place where the weather was pleasant nearly all the time, and there was field work available in the harvest fields during the summer months. Again, it must have been a decision born of desperation that caused them to consider yet another move. This one, however, was intended to be temporary. As so many Mid-westerners did during the '30's and '40's, the plan was to make the journey to the Central Valley of California, work in the fields for a couple of months, and then return home to Eastern Kansas. They left two married children behind in Kansas, and there were now grandchildren, as well as a congregation of church people who loved and wanted them back. Their ties to Fredonia were strong.

Going West

Chapter Eight

The trip to California was similar, according to my husband, to the sojourn experienced by so many displaced farmers and chronicled in the well-known story, <u>The Grapes of Wrath</u>. They would need two vehicles and a small trailer to carry the family and a few necessities, which would include Mom's cook stove. However, there would be no farm equipment since the move was only expected be for a few months.

This trip would prove to be a challenge. They got as far as Colorado before a major breakdown occurred and one vehicle had to be overhauled. Thankfully, they had friends and extended family in the area, and therefore were given lodging for the night. As soon as the repairs were made, it was back on the road again. Another challenge was the post-war speed limit of thirty-five miles per hour. Being a law-abiding citizen, Dad set the pace at thirty-five, but the second vehicle, an older car cut down into a pickup truck, was driven by the eldest of the three sons still at home. He had just turned sixteen and acquired a driver's license only a few days earlier, so he was a relatively new driver and was pulling a trailer at that. This was hardly the safest situation considering the poor road conditions in some places and the hair-pin curves that would face them in the California mountains. Boys being boys, they finally figured out how to get a little more speed than the 35 miles per hour set by Dad; they would slow down until the lead car was out of vision, then enjoy driving faster to catch up again.

Unfortunately, this plan back-fired when their vehicle came to a grinding halt beside the road and refused to go another foot! With the family car disappearing off in the distance and with no phone service or help of any kind, the boys simply sat there until Dad finally realized they were not following. When they could not be seen in the rearview mirror, he had no choice but to turn around, go back and find them. The boys had not anticipated that what seemed like fun at the time could turn into a problem. And of course, the parents would not have been pleased over the delay. The breakdown couldn't be fixed on the roadside, however, and it required returning to the nearest town to have some major repair work done.

While this presented a troubling challenge that was time consuming and costly for the parents, to the children it was a pleasant break in the constant logging of miles. According to my husband, their dad booked a night's lodging at a hotel in town, and it would prove to be the one and only night the family ever spent in a hotel. The children, of course, thought this was an exciting diversion, but it was an unexpected expense for the parents. Since the children were used to sleeping three to a bed at home, they probably crowded into two or three rooms. A hotel was different than staying with relatives or just pulling to the side of the road for some exercise and a short rest, and it was an experience my husband still remembers fondly.

Willis recalls very little of the rest of the trip until finally late one night the two vehicles pulled into the yard of Preacher Abe Koehn's dairy farm in Winton, California. The Koehns also had a large family and lived in a relatively old farmhouse, but people in those days were always willing to share what they had, and share they did. Children were scattered around on blankets on the floor, and everyone slept the sleep of exhaustion. In the morning, the Nichols family eagerly moved into the house Preacher Abe had rented for them near Atwater. Knowing Mom's industrious ways, there must have been much scrubbing and cleaning as the three bedroom house WITH BATH was prepared for its new occupants. Having an indoor bathroom was a new experience, a luxury that must have been especially welcome to the female members of the family.

It wasn't long before Dad found work in the carpentry trade, and soon money was coming in. Also, it was harvest time in California. Picking and cutting peaches, grapes, and other fruit, along with similar kinds of farm labor gave this large family an opportunity to earn the money that would sustain them in their new home. It was expected that all those old enough to work in the fields would do so in order to pay off debts accumulated during the hard times they had gone through. This would have included Mom and four or five of the older children.

I have often wondered how long it took for the family to adjust to the conveniences of California living and put aside the notion that they would return home to Kansas. The family settled in with the local church, the Holdeman Mennonite congregation at Winton,

California, where Dad was invited to share the pulpit with ministers already established there. It is the policy in Holdeman churches to have several ministers who rotate preaching responsibilities from Sunday to Sunday. One minister gives the introduction, another delivers the main message, and the third gives the "addition" which usually includes his thoughts on the subject of the main sermon. This takes place both Sunday morning and evening, with the ministers taking turns as they feel led. The clergy is unpaid, so the minister/father in the home is expected to earn the living for the family by working at a job or on his own farm or dairy.

Some time after they decided to make California their permanent home, Dad built a home on Winton Way about three miles north of the small town of Winton, giving the family the opportunity to move into a new house. It was a simple home with two bedrooms on the ground floor and with an additional large bedroom in the basement especially for the boys. This home is where my husband spent some of his important growing up years. It was the house they lived in when he went to high school for one year until he was sixteen. It was also the property on which Dad would establish a goat dairy, and where my husband was expected to do the milking. Both Dad and Mom were hard-working individuals, and in the summer, Mom frequently worked at a cannery nearby. When he could, Dad picked up work as a carpenter.

After a number of years, the Nichols family was invited by the congregation at Livingston to move to the Livingston community and help with the church there. They were offered a home on Peach Ave about three miles west of town. This property had a large barn, giving Dad the opportunity to operate a small dairy. The house was inadequate with only two bedrooms, but there was another small structure on the property which the boys could use as their bedroom. It was while the family lived on this property that the younger children married and left home, leaving Mom and Dad to began their "Golden Years" with just the two of them.

Dad and Mom missed having their own home, and after a few years the children pulled together to purchase a home for them about a mile away on Washington Blvd. This would be their home until the time of Dad's sudden passing from a heart attack in 1968. Mom was devastated and didn't see how she could survive. She continued to live out in the country for a time, giving various granddaughters the opportunity to come spend nights with her to keep her company. After awhile the family sold that home and purchased one for her within walking distance of the church. Here she appreciated having her family visit and once again she raised a small garden. This was something she enjoyed and was familiar with, having gardened all her life. She was well into her nineties when the family decided Mom should no longer live by herself. Her final years were spent in Grace Nursing Home where she resided until the time of her death, lacking only a few months from reaching 100 years of age.

GETTING MARRIED

Chapter Nine

Willis and I got married so young that it's hard to believe our parents supported our decision, but they did. I graduated from high school in June, and we got married in October, just a few days before my 18th birthday. Willis was twenty and would need to have his parents sign for him, so my mom thought it might be less embarrassing for him if my parents also needed to sign, which would not be the case when I reached eighteen. Their signatures on our license made everything legal, and so we were all set. I had sewn my wedding dress, a light blue sheer wool fabric, which was a bit chancy since it could have been very warm on October 19, although, with the wedding starting at 10:30, we still enjoyed the coolness of the morning.

The little wooden church in which we married held perhaps 100 worshipers, and the basement, normally used for children's Sunday School classes, would be adequate for the reception. This would follow immediately after the ceremony and would not only include serving a meal but also the opening and viewing of the wedding gifts, a tradition that was meaningful for the ladies, particularly. The simplicity of the wedding made everything easier—there was no decorating of the sanctuary or the basement, no flowers, no wedding cake, nothing that could be considered "prideful" and therefore inappropriate. On our wedding day, we would both get ready at our individual homes, then Willis would pick me up at the designated time and drive both of us to the church. There we would stand in the back of the sanctuary, waiting for the first verse of "Tread Softly," the traditional Holdeman wedding song, to be sung. During the second verse we would walk together down the aisle to the front pew, sit next to each other on the "women's side," and the service would continue similar to the usual pattern.

It began with an "introduction" by one of the ministers who welcomed everyone, followed by a prayer for which the entire congregation would turn around and kneel at their pew, followed by another song and then the wedding message. Since Willis's father was a minister, he brought the message and performed the ceremony for Willis and me. Generally the message was based on a Scripture that would have something to do with the need for love and forgiveness in the home, and the importance of the husband being the spiritual leader. The wife's role was to be the supporter of her husband and keeper of the home. Sometimes much emphasis was placed on the need for "submission" of the wife and her role in the marriage. She was to trust God in the divine order of marriage and certainly never usurp her husband's place. Even though not all young men were leaders by temperament or training, spiritual or otherwise, this order was the Biblical pattern and was never questioned.

My new husband and I were happy to finally be together without feeling guilty, and our brief honeymoon to the California coast was an enjoyable experience. Just the simple pleasure of being together was a privilege, and we entered married life with a lot of enthusiasm. My parents had given us twenty acres of open land that included a small, two-room house situated near the road on the west side of the property, and we were eager to set up housekeeping. This was, of course, a generous gift and rather unusual. We had expected to do what other newly married couples did, which was find a house to rent and move in. However, my father was of the belief that establishing one's own home was the best way to start, and we felt very privileged that they were financially able to help us in this way. My father also bought a milk cow for Willis, although I don't remember that this was something we really wanted. However, Willis milked the cow and we sold grade B milk, which helped us buy groceries.

I was now a "homemaker," and the fact that my housekeeping skills were rather limited did not seem to be a problem. After all, who couldn't take care of a small, two-room house and cook a few meals! My cooking skills were composed of a few simple dishes that I had made for my family as a teenager, but I was willing to learn. After all, I had a cookbook, and having hamburgers one day and spaghetti the next, with an occasional creamed tuna on toast didn't faze my new husband. With the passage of time and my growing desire to become a good cook, meals became much more appealing as I tried various other dishes. I did take pride in being a "good wife," and cooking was an important part of it.

Cleaning was less appealing, especially since I was an avid reader, and without my mom nearby to pull me out of my reading reveries, I quickly learned how to survive with the most simple of skills in that department. Pulling up the covers of the bed was almost as good as "making" it, and putting dishes in the sink almost as good as washing them. I had a friend who did the "sweeping and dusting thing" every day, and that seemed a waste of time to me. Who would ever notice? Cleaning house didn't give me the satisfaction that it apparently did some of my friends, and was done sporadically at best. Occasionally my long-suffering husband would take care of the dirty dishes, and I was so willing to let him. This did not fit in with the assumption that all Mennonite women were immaculate housekeepers, but I did try to make sure that if "company was coming," everything looked neat and tidy, at least on the surface.

It wasn't long before I got very bored at being home all day with little to do. Willis took our only car to work, so unless someone picked me up, I had no choice but to stay home. When I was offered a job at the high school as secretary to the principal, I gladly took it. It gave me a chance to get out and about, make friends with the other office staff, and earn some money. That fact that I had limited skills as a secretary apparently didn't figure into the hiring, and I was a fairly quick learner. I had one semester of bookkeeping in high school and one of "office practice," which meant I could run the copy machine. I had also learned to type, and answering the phone comes pretty naturally to any female, so I was all set. I do believe I took notes as the principal dictated letters I was to write for him, but inexperienced as I was, they must have been fairly simple.

When Willis received his draft papers in the mail informing him that his number had been called up, we sprang into action. Our Holdeman people did not serve in the military, and it became imperative to get his status changed as quickly as possible from 1-A, which meant "Active duty," to C.O., which stood for Conscientious Objector. That meant that even though our boys would spend two years working in government service, it would not be in the army. The problem was to convince a judge that Willis was serious about his anti-war objections and that he could not morally use a weapon to kill another human being, even in wartime.

While Willis was a church member, his commitment to the doctrines of the church was minimal at best. By personality, he was easy-going and he certainly did not want to attend basic training and try to fit into a lifestyle—army life—that was so foreign to his upbringing. The children in our families were taught to be non-violent, and generally speaking, there was little physical fighting going on in Mennonite homes, even among the children. Yes, boys did a fair amount of scuffling in their younger years, but I did not know anyone who took this so far as to seriously injure a brother or cousin. That would not have been acceptable. I don't know at what age children realized that young men in our culture did not join the army or any military establishment, but not everyone had heart-felt convictions regarding this position. Even boys who chose not to become church members usually had this mind-set established because of family and church teaching. Still, there were certain young men who broke tradition and did join the army, particularly if they had been drafted before another classification was acquired. Several went as non-combatants, which put them into some sort of medical service. But for church members to go into the military of any kind would not be tolerated by the church and would terminate their membership.

As it turned out, Willis did receive his notice of induction into the army and had to scramble to reverse that classification. His boss and his pastor both wrote letters to the draft board to let them know that they had confidence in Willis's stand as a conscientious objector and asked that his classification should be reversed. At the very last moment, the official reversal of classification came and he was identified as a C.O. or conscientious objector. He could go into alternative service.

MOVING TO THE BIG CITY

Chapter Ten

It was quite an adventure for two farm kids when we realized that we were actually moving to the big city of Los Angeles in Southern California for two years while Willis fulfilled his service to his country. The problem was that I had taken a job as secretary to the principal at Livingston High School, and having just started, it was difficult to announce that I would now be leaving. So we figured out a plan in which Willis would go at the designated time and I would wait until the school year was over, then I would join him. My brother Gene and I went with him on the trip to Los Angles and helped find an apartment along the beach front of Venice, a suburb of L.A. Then the two of us, my brother and I, came home on the bus, one that stopped at every little burg along the way. My hope of going frequently to visit him lost its appeal by the length of that bus trip, but as it turned out, it didn't matter anyway.

I had my own problems at home. I began having nightmares and walking in my sleep in the guest bedroom of my parents' home and calling out for my husband. My mother felt sorry for me and perhaps got tired of me disturbing her sleep. I soon was convinced that I "needed" to support my husband and be by his side. A replacement had already been found for my secretarial position, and all that was required at this point was to move up the date of her starting time and for me to gracefully depart. So, after only a month or two of living alone, Willis was joined by a very willing wife to begin this new life in the city.

Our first home was only a half block from the beach, which for two kids from Central California seemed like a dream come true. We thought it would be wonderful to be so close to the ocean and we expected we would play in the water and on the sandy beach frequently. However, we found that something so readily available loses much of its appeal. With Willis gone during the work day, I did the usual housekeeping chores, laundry, and cooking, and our walks on the beach happened only occasionally. In my spare time, loving to read and having found the location of the library, books filled my days. I also enjoyed visiting with other young wives of the Holdeman Mennonite boys who had come for "voluntary service" although without a second car that was challenging. Farm girls don't know how to use city buses very well.

It wasn't long before we began looking for a "real" house, one that was on a regular street where we actually had a place to park our car and also that had a real bedroom, not just a sofa that opened up. Soon we found a "house in the back," which is how nearly all of our friends lived, also. The house in front would be the larger, more impressive house, while the one on the back of the lot would be a small, one-bedroom home that may have been the "first home" of the owners when they were younger. It became quite a joke among our group that we all lived in "the house in the back," reaffirming that our low-income status was shared by all. Of course, the rental prices of houses in the back were much better and more affordable. The house we moved into, which we considered our first real home in West Los Angeles, was $59.50 per month. It was a low rate, but was still a challenge for us to be able to make that monthly payment as well as other living expenses, including medical needs. Willis received a check of about $160 per month, which had to be stretched quite a bit to cover basic expenses such as food, gas for the car, and later, medical bills. There was no money in the budget for non-essentials, and I remember buying shoes as a "birthday gift" at one point because it was the only way we could justify even necessary items.

It was while we lived here that my husband came home once in the middle of the day with a black eye and other cuts and bruises. The boys worked in the mental wards of the V.A. Hospital on Wilshire Blvd in West Los Angeles before the days of tranquillizers, so with minimal medical treatment there would occasionally be some agitation among the patients. On this particular day one of the patients had jumped Willis from the back, knocked him down, and proceeded to stomp him. Fortunately, another patient came to his rescue, or the story might have ended quite differently. He had a black eye and other bruises, but was able to be up and about, so back to work he went the next day. I, however, had misgivings. I did not want to lose a husband because there was not enough help to provide protection when the inmates got violent.

The two years spent in West Los Angeles were good in many ways. We started growing up and taking responsibility for making our time there both meaningful and useful. Our local congregations back home rented a house for our unit in which to have church services, which would consist of singing and Sunday school on days when we did not have a guest minister. At least once a month an ordained minister would come from one of the two nearest congregations, Livingston or Winton, California. The second year Willis and I rented a house only a few blocks from the first house which had an extra bedroom and was available for out-of-town visitors, particularly visiting ministers. It was always enjoyable to have these guests. My parents had been very hospitable during my growing up years, so it seemed quite natural for me to have over-night guests. By this time I had learned to cook a variety of dishes, and breakfast for my overnight guests was not a difficult challenge. My homemade biscuits were light and fluffy, and I'd gathered other tasty recipes from friends and was now cooking delectable meals.

The big and life-changing event during our time in L.A. was the birth of our precious first child, a daughter we named Michalene Gale, born in Santa Monica Hospital only a few miles away. Because my mother had passed on her love of babies to me, I had no doubt that I could be a good mother, even though I was only nineteen years old at her birth. Fortunately, my mother came down to L.A to give us a hand. It was a five hour drive from the farming community of Livingston, so she couldn't just pop in when she got the notion. She stayed with us for a week, which was a life-saver, and she informed me that she had come, not to take over the baby care, but to cook and do laundry and clean so that I could totally enjoy our new little one. And enjoy her we did. Willis was on swing shift at that time and would be coming home shortly after eleven pm., and he would sit and hold her and talk to her before we all went to bed. Our obstetrician sent out his visiting nurse, and she reported that I was the one who had "a commonsense mother," and that all three of us were doing well. This was truly a special time, and watching our precious little girl grow and flourish was an incredible blessing.

Of course, we were not the only ones who gave birth to their first child in L.A. Soon our group of service couples had about six or seven darling little ones to admire and enjoy. As mothers we would help the new mother by cooking dinner or washing clothes for them. We would also check with each other for advice and to see how each little one grew and developed, making our group there a "community within a community."

Our service commitment was two years, and soon our time in Los Angles was winding down. The time came when different couples would pack up and return to their homes in Kansas, Oklahoma, Idaho or California, leaving an empty place in our group. It wasn't long until we also, my husband and I, began to make plans to return home, although somewhat reluctantly. We had grown to love the small communities in which we lived and to enjoy the balmy Los Angeles weather. The two years during which we had served in "voluntary service" had been beneficial to us. We had bonded as a group of "misplaced Holdeman Mennonites," away from our usual farming communities and transplanted into a city environment so foreign to us. We had learned how to take care of ourselves and each other and had built ties that would last a lifetime. We also know that the caring attitudes of our young men were a blessing to the veterans being cared for, and that they had benefited from the service of these young men, inexperienced though they were. We came from various states to serve our country, and our young husbands met an important need as aids in a veteran's medical facility. But now it was time to return to life in our own communities and to resume life as we knew it. Reluctantly, we packed up and moved back home.

BACK TO LIFE ON THE FARM

Chapter Eleven

Coming home for us meant resettling in the little house in Livingston we had left two years earlier. We were now a family of three, with our first child, whom we nicknamed "Micki," about nine months old. The little two-room house was certainly adequate for the three of us, and learning to fit back into the farming community was relatively simple. It was the life we knew.

The first item of necessity, of course, was a source of income. Willis had done some farm work for various employers and had generally earned minimum wages, but it wasn't long before he was looking for something a bit more stable. My dad had a friend in Winton who ran a machine shop, and when he asked that his son-in-law be given a chance to learn the welding trade, the owner was agreeable. When Willis first went to work there he had never held a welder in his hand, but it didn't take long for him to get the hang of it, and soon he had a dependable job welding farm machinery together and being successful in a trade.

At the same time, we did have the twenty acre farm that had not been developed but did have access to irrigation water. During the years that Willis worked as a welder, he also farmed on the side, gaining experience with each passing season. One year when he planted sweet potatoes, the price was low and we barely broke even. Another time he grew watermelons, raising a bumper crop of large and luscious melons, only to have to dump them when the market for melons tanked. Another time he bought a bean cutter and did some custom cutting of the vines of back-eyed peas, a row crop common during that time. He would get up very early and do his custom cutting in the field, after which he went to his job as a welder. He worked hard to provide for his growing family.

After being home in Livingston for a number of months, I became pregnant with our second child, our first little boy! With two children, our small house was inadequate. However, while I was still in the early stages of pregnancy, my parents came to the rescue and helped us plan and build a new house on our property. Of course, we had little or no extra money to invest, but by selling and moving off our small, two room house, we had a little money to contribute. Fortunately, houses didn't cost that much to build in 1956, and we had an uncle who, along with his son-in-law, needed work. My dad hired them, and we soon had framework going up that would become our new home. This was very exciting for us, and because of our limited resources we were quite frugal in the planning of this home. We didn't need rugs for the floor when linoleum would work, and the furniture we were given was hand-me-downs, such as the old dinning room set that my parents no longer needed. Especially heart-warming was the small wooden table and chairs that my parents had began their own housekeeping with so many years earlier. We knew how privileged we were to actually be the owners of a new three-bedroom house only four years into our marriage. We were so grateful to our parents for this great opportunity, knowing that we would have spent years saving up to be able to build a home on our own.

It began to appear that the completion of the house and the pending birth of our second child would coincide, and I started to scheme on how I could give birth and still be part of the moving-in process. Our only option was to move before I went into labor, which could be at any time. And so I began to carry over small things such as clothes and household items while Willis moved the heavier stuff, some with help from a friend or family member. We didn't have a working toilet in the new house yet and had to go back into the old house for that, but soon we were settled in quite well. We did have a bathtub and kitchen appliances, so we could bathe and I could cook. The bedroom was furnished with the bed and dresser we'd bought shortly after marriage, which had stayed in the small house while we were in L.A. The floor coverings were not yet laid, but the sub flooring was in so we could walk on the floors. We knew that with patience we would complete each project, and all things essential to living in our new home would come with time. And so we moved in. Within a couple of days our new baby arrived and we became a family of four. We were very happy for our new little one, a son we named Bruce, who would become "Daddy's little helper" down the road in a few years.

Regarding our spiritual lives, Willis and I were always very consistent in our church attendance during our entire time in the Holdeman church. We were still young, and I would presume that our walk with the Lord was shallow, mostly following what we had been taught without being truly grounded in the Word of God by personal convictions. As with any member in a conservative church, we had questions now and then, but our lifestyle was pleasant and comfortable, and our desire was to grow and become stronger in our faith. Having guests and visiting other families within the church was an activity both my husband and I enjoyed. We connected with other young families who were also getting started in life and raising a family, and we enjoyed visiting in the homes of both the Koehn and Nichols relatives. Getting together to show off our new babies was exciting for us as with all new parents. Fortunately, we were blessed with good health and a reasonably good source of income from Willis's job. There was rarely any extra money, but we were able to pay our bills and take little trips now and then. We were never involved in "worldly entertainment" which meant that our income was spent frugally on the essentials of caring for a family. All in all, we were a happy couple with much to be thankful for.

Never in our wildest dreams would we have imagined that the time would come when we would no longer be actively engaged in this secure and supportive church community. Even though we were "set apart" from the larger community in which we lived, we had a support system through our church that would stand by us and help us should we ever have serious difficulties or go through hard times. Yes, we had a "rule-driven" lifestyle, but we were accustomed to a life with restrictions that would keep us safe from the sinful world out there. Our church people put much confidence in the fact that our simple, Bible-based way of life kept us protected from many of the problems faced by others in the culture around us.

OUR CHURCH
CONFERENCE, 1959

Chapter Twelve

The birth of our third baby was a happy occasion, and we began to feel like a "real family" now as a family of five, the parents of three small children. I loved the role of being a mother, and Willis was a kind and loving father. Also, day by day he was working to develop our farm so that it would be more productive and would provide for our growing family. We were strong Holdemans, and when it came time for the gathering of the membership of all the congregations in a church-wide conference, we made the decision to go. This was before the days of air conditioned cars or car seats for babies and toddlers, so we piled our two youngest in the back seat with books and various small toys and the baby, as always, sat on my lap. Looking back, we know now that it was not a safe situation, but this was the generally accepted method of family travel in 1959, and we were excited to go.

I remember the opening service, especially the vigorous singing of hymns that focused on the glorious church of Jesus, which, of course, we all agreed was our own church. It was a good feeling to belong to the "one true visible church," first begun, as we believed, in the establishment of the early church in the account in the Book of Acts. Of course, we knew that our particular denomination was "called out" from the larger Mennonite Church because "the mother church" had fallen into decay. We believed that God had used John Holdeman, a sincere and conservative member of the Mennonite church, to take a stand and draw attention to certain areas where the church had become lax. He believed that "the Candlestick of Truth," which had been handed down from the apostles' time had grown dim, and that in spite of his sincere and continuing reproof, the leaders of the Mennonite church did not heed his cry for a new reformation. Two areas which he felt were being overlooked were the need for stronger and more effective child discipline policies and for a harsher and more stringent stand on excommunication and holding the avoidance. If properly carried out, he believed, this should be a firm and unyielding separation from other church members, family and friends alike. The idea was that the avoidance should be so painful for the disobedient member that he would not be able to bear up under the pressure and would repent and return to the fold. Therefore, it seemed justified that the excommunicated could no longer eat at the same table, nor could they shake hands with friends and family who came to visit. The goal was to bring anyone who strayed back to forgiveness and re-acceptance.

Even though very few followed his line of thinking in the beginning, slowly over time it drew members who supported his views. Having begun in 1859, we had now come to the eve of the 1950's and had reached 1959, the centennial of the Holdeman movement. The original group of two had now grown to several thousand members with congregations scattered over the United States and Canada. But while the followers of John Holdeman still saw themselves as Mennonites and claimed that heritage, other Mennonite groups saw them as an off-shoot who had stepped into a more legalistic way of life. Holdeman Mennonites did not take communion with other Mennonite groups nor did they offer their own communion fellowship to them. And while other Mennonite groups also held to many of the convictions of the Holdemans such as no involvement in military service, no participation in politics, no voting or campaigning, and living a plain, simple lifestyle, the Holdemans tended to be a bit more conservative on most issues. While other Mennonite groups even went so far as to establish their own Christian colleges, the Holdemans believed any kind of higher education was wrong and would lead to pride, and was therefore forbidden. Holdemans taught that while one must be obedient to civil laws, which demanded an eighth grade education in some states and staying in school until age sixteen in other states, college wasn't even a consideration. College couldn't be a Christian institution; any college claiming to be so was misguided.

Having made the decision to go to conference, we set out on the trip from California to Kansas and the Lone Tree congregation, a large church established in a central location, the place where conferences were held. For a young family with three small children, this was a serious undertaking and one that required three days of driving with stops only for an occasional meal and a night's sleep at a motel somewhere. We were eager to experience this gathering of the membership from congregations scattered throughout the United States and Canada. We were confident of the spiritual linage that proved our church was the true church, but we also needed to experience the affirmation that our denomination was truly the only church built upon such a divine foundation.

As with many other visitors from a distance, we had extended family in the area and greatly appreciated being able to spend nights with them during the conference. We were also very excited to be in Kansas, the state of my husband's birthplace. But it was the purpose of our coming, to reinforce our belief in our church's divine calling of being the one and only true church that was especially significant. Sunday came, and we were eager for the first meeting to begin. With three little children to care for during the services, it meant we both spent time in the respective "baby rooms," me with the littlest one on the women's side, and Willis with our two-year-old son on the men's side. Our eldest daughter, who was now five years old, usually sat with my mother; the two had a strong bond and Grandma usually had pencil and paper to write on and a handkerchief with which to make various play items by folding and tying it just so.

On the first day the issue of the head covering was introduced for discussion. Many of the younger women had discovered that sewing two seams on the sides and making the triangle of material into a sort of cap was simpler and easier to wear during the day. Most women did not wear the covering tied under the chin on everyday as they did for church; they wanted a more comfortable way to wear it at home or when they went to town. Turning the triangle into a cap made it easier for young girls and older women who might have difficulty attaching the covering with many bobby pins and to tuck in the edges to make a neat looking cap. I had recently purchased such a cap for myself and did find it to be neater and simpler. But was this acceptable or was it moving away from the old style that had been worn for many years? Trying something "new" was always suspect. The importance of the "prayer covering" was paramount, especially since it was one of the symbols that identified our particular denomination. Some called us "the black cap Mennonites."

As the discussion began, I was amazed that there were strong opinions on both sides of the issue. It became obvious that these two seams were no small thing. Most of the speaking was done by various ministers, but since this was also a women's issue, I believe several minister's wives were invited to share their points of view. I recall that those who worked in nursing homes with elderly Holdeman women pleaded for the acceptance of the cap to make it easier to groom these older women. Eventually the vote was taken by the delegates who had voting privileges, and the cap was rejected. As I remember, the primary reason was that it was moving away from the old way of doing things and the fear was that it might lead to more, and perhaps less desirable, changes.

For Willis and me this whole discussion was unsettling. That evening when we got to our bedroom, we looked at each other and said, "People are dying in many places in our world without ever hearing the Gospel, and we are expending our energy on the problem of whether two seams should be allowed in the everyday head covering?" Why were we quibbling about unessential issues while life and death issues were set aside?

The following day the question of the tape recorder and whether it should be allowed came up. This was a helpful device many of the missionaries were using to learn the languages of the people with whom they worked. They found it extremely helpful in their efforts to communicate with those who neither spoke or understood English, and they literally pleaded their case before the conference. When they saw they were losing ground in their quest to be allowed to use it, they then asked if exceptions could be made for mission field use only. This was considered, but in the end it was decided that any use at all could only lead to unapproved use such as taping group singing in homes and also buying tapes, possibly of other "so-called Christians," that were questionable to say the least. My husband, spending much time in the men's baby room, thought it quite paradoxical that all the while this rather passionate discussion was going on, the entire conference was being taped on a recorder in the baby room.

However, even while we had questions about certain concerns, there were many things about conference we enjoyed, particularly the singing and the fellowship. We made new friends and enjoyed being a part of something that seemed to be a strong organization based on

Leona Koehn Nichols

the Word of God and supportive of the teachings with which we had been brought up. It was an experience we valued, but it had also been revealing. We somehow assumed that in being "the one true visible church," the leaders were divinely led and since our Heavenly Father was not confused or at variance with these issues, neither would His people on earth be. I suppose the humanness of opposing views was unsettling to anyone with unrealistic expectations. We certainly had no intention to make any kind of drastic move, and as time progressed, we dealt with issues as we always had—with careful consideration, but by trusting our leadership.

Decision-Making in Our Family

Chapter Thirteen

In the meantime, we had a family to raise, a family that kept growing in size. We had three children when we went to our church conference, and life was good for our small family. I was very thankful for my mother, who loved my children and was able to baby-sit when I needed that kind of help. I even took a part-time job working as a bookkeeper for our local doctor, the one who had delivered baby number three, a little girl we named Bethany, in the doctor's office instead of the hospital. That was the closest we could come to a home birth, and with the help of a younger cousin, I was able to care for my older children and our new baby. By delivering in the doctor's office, Willis had been able to share this birth experience during a time when husbands were not allowed in the delivery room. This was meaningful to both of us and drew our family even closer together.

Unexpectedly, and to our deep sadness, my mother passed away between our daughter Bethany's birth and the birth of our fourth child, a son we named Daniel. This was an incredible loss. She was a grandmother who loved children and had been a confidante and support to me as a young mother. Her passing was so unexpected, and happened after only a couple of days in the hospital. Our family, as well as the families of my two brothers, was devastated, and learning to live without her was painful. We had always known that my mother was unusual in the exuberance with which she lived life and her willingness to lend a helping hand wherever it was needed. I was angry with God. I knew He could have healed her and allowed her to continue her life of service to so many. I saw others who made little contribution to ministering to the needs of others, and it simply made no sense. She was only fifty-seven. I grieved the loss, not only for myself but for the children who would not know their grandmother.

Now, as the only daughter, I was overwhelmed with the sense of being left with a monumental task of carrying out what I supposed were her wishes with the things she had left behind. What would she want done, and to whom would she want me to donate the things she valued? As I napped one day a few weeks after her death, she was suddenly there in my room, sitting on the bed beside me. I was startled and I said, "Mom, is it really you?"

She smiled, but did not speak. Then I thought, "I know how I can tell—I will feel her dress, and if it's the same starched cotton she always wore, I will know for sure." And it was. I rubbed the fabric between my fingers and knew it was my mom in one of her everyday dresses.

She sat there just looking at me and smiling for some time, and then she got up to go, moving toward the door. I cried out, "Oh, Mom, please don't go. There are so many things I need to ask you. I don't know what to do with your things!"

She didn't speak but she just smiled. Then amazingly, I heard her words, although they were not spoken aloud.

"Don't worry about my things, Honey. They're just things." And she slipped through the door and was gone. I can still see this event in my mind these many years later, and that truth still echoes in my heart— things are just things and not of eternal value. They won't matter at all in the life of our future. What a comfort that was to me.

As a mother of a growing family, life was much more difficult without my mother's helping hand as babies four, five and six arrived. However, we were compensated somewhat by the assistance our older children gave in helping the younger ones during playtime and when we went away somewhere. This was a practice common in large families, and it was good training in learning responsibility. We were a family who helped each other, and we built the love and respect for one another that has held through the passing years. Even though today our children are grown and have families of their own, the family love that we still enjoy began when they were precious babies.

A few years after Danny's birth, we were blessed with a daughter, Darlisa, followed a few years later by our last child, a son named Jon. We were pleased and so appreciative to God for the lovely family we had and were very conscious of our responsibilities as parents. Scripture teaches that we are to "nurture our children in the admonition of the Lord," and that was truly our sincere desire. Six precious little ones God had placed in our care, and while we were busy, we knew God would give the strength and wisdom we needed to accomplish the task. We were bringing them up, not only for this life but for eternity. We have never ceased being thankful for our incredible children, each one a blessing and a gift from God.

Caring for them and providing for their needs was a task we found doable. They were all children who wanted to please their parents and who were pleasant in the company of adults as well as their friends. Of course we were not perfect parents, no one ever is, but we knew our ultimate goal was to teach them about Jesus and to encourage them to give their lives to Him. To this end we attempted to live faithful lives before them and to make sure they knew the Bible stories and spiritual principles so essential to choosing to live for God. Regular church attendance was a given, and the conversation in our home was generally kind and encouraging.

However, we were a Holdeman family, and decisions regarding our children and what they could or could not do as children in a conservative family of Believers came up periodically. Some choices could be determined by our own convictions, but many were decided either in members' meetings by majority vote or by our ministers' personal recommendations. Certain situations might be given some leeway for personal opinion while others were not. For example, when our third child entered kindergarten, she came home all excited one day and very eager to share her news.

"Mamma, Mamma," she said with great enthusiasm, "There is this thing at school called a piano. Please, Mamma, can we get one?

"Oh, no, Honey," I replied, "I'm so sorry but we can't."

"Why not, Mamma?" she asked, and I wondered how to explain it to her.

"Sweetheart, we can't have a piano because our church thinks we might do something wrong with it." (How do you explain doctrine to a five year old?)

And with her eyes filling with tears, she said, "But Mamma, God knows I would never do anything wrong with it." Her innocence was compelling, and even at age five she knew that it was God we wanted to please. But it was our church to which we were accountable, and so some options were off the table.

These were the challenges we faced as we tried to explain the fact that our church did not allow musical instruments, or photographs, or radios or TV's or many of the things that were commonplace in the homes of school friends. As they got older they picked up on what was allowed and what was not, and they accepted these rules just as we, their parents had many years earlier. Lifestyles and church principles are usually "caught" more than "taught,' and while there are many "unwritten" rules in conservative churches, most children know at an early age what is permissible and what is not.

With each consecutive school year there would be decisions to be made and limitations to be explained. My husband and I did not think much of the answer, "Because the church says so." We wanted to give them the spiritual principle that was based on the Bible, but in some cases there simply wasn't one. This was true when we dealt with what was supposed to be a special treat for sixth graders called "Sixth Grade Camp." It was school policy to provide sixth-graders with the privilege of getting on a bus, along with a number of teachers and parents, to go up to a camp in the mountains for five days of "Outdoor Education" in the middle of the week. When our daughter came home with a permission slip that needed to be signed in order for her to go, we had a decision to make. This was a special event when students would be exposed to the beauties of nature in the beautiful Sierra Nevada Mountains just to the east of us. It was an issue that, to my knowledge, had not come up for discussion in our council meetings. I did not think there was a hard and fast rule.

We had been a camping family since our second child was born, but we always went with cousins and friends who were also Holdemans. For many of us here in California, taking the family camping up in the beautiful Sierras or out on the coast for a few days was an inexpensive way to enjoy some vacation time, and our children loved the experience. We would buy, rent or borrow tents and sleeping bags, set a destination where we would meet other family members, and together have a lovely time enjoying the outdoors. Because most Holdemans love to sing, an activity that is not only acceptable but encouraged, sitting around the campfire in the evening and singing rounds and some of our favorite hymns, all a Capella, of course, was so meaningful for us. This is truly one of our family's treasured memories.

So when our daughter became a sixth grader, we had no objection to her going with her school friends to enjoy a similar experience. However, many of our church people saw it differently. To them, it was allowing our children to be away from home in the company of non-believers who might influence them negatively. The whole idea just didn't "feel right" to them. And so, very reluctantly, we chose not to allow our daughter to participate in this activity. She was disappointed but compliant; we, however, were not happy about the situation. We had capitulated, but it was not the choice we would have made on our own. To us it sounded like fun and surely was an innocent event that our daughter would have enjoyed.

Three years later, the same situation came up for our eldest son, and once again, we wondered just how rigid this ruling was. It was not a conference decision, after all, nor was it a formal decision made by our local church. It was one of many things that were just "understood." Again, our decision was to comply with the practice of our church and to not let him go. He and another Holdeman boy in his class spent the entire week very bored and being sent to the library for the day since the sixth grade class was away at camp. He still remembers how frustrating this was for him, particularly since he had grown up going family camping and knowing how enjoyable that was. He also remembers wanting to be on the baseball team and not being allowed. Again, not a church rule on the books, but we all knew that our children were not to participate in "worldly" things. Even though our children were compliant and wanted to please us, there was also this aspect of "missing out" on certain privileges average American children enjoyed. Like all parents, we wanted our children to enjoy the advantages that come with living the middle class lifestyle in America. We didn't enjoy saying "no" to harmless activities.

With our third child this changed, and from this point on, our remaining children were allowed to go to sixth grade camp, which they remember fondly. Our third child, our middle daughter, also remembers that it was the first time she was allowed to wear jeans just like her classmates. Dresses were the norm, of course, but we made an exception for "outdoor education." The clothes issue is big in the Holdeman church, and girls are always expected to wear plain, simple dresses that have been sewn at home by their mothers. These are usually quite conservative in style and needed to be long enough to cover the knee. The pattern and fabric should not be loud or designed to build "pride" in the young girl wearing it.

For our fourth child and second son, this positive opportunity to attend sixth grade camp came just after a very difficult experience with his best friends at school, all children of Holdeman parents. They had come to him one day on the playground to tell him that they could no longer play with him. This was hard for them, as well as for our son, and the one who told him was crying as he did so. I don't know just how they explained it, but it was due to the stand his parents were taking regarding our conflict with the church. It seems the fact that we were out of favor in our church extended to our children and they had apparently been told by their parents that they, their children, needed to separate themselves from our children. Usually the avoidance, as it is called, is practiced only on those who were actually members and have become deviant, but in this case, no doubt because of the severity of the charges against us, this alienation needed to filter down to our young children as well. Fortunately, our two youngest were young enough that they had not yet made close Holdeman friends, and therefore did not go through that particular trauma. In fact, by the time they were in the sixth grade, we were no longer members.

I am sure there were many such issues that arose, most of which we had no trouble with compliance. However, there were some subjects that were made a church mandate, and then there was no option. For example, my girls had always gone to school with their hair in braids, just as I had done as a child, and this was still acceptable when my eldest daughter became a church member. Soon, however, a family from Kansas moved into the area with very strong convictions about female believers wearing the head covering to school, especially during junior high and high school. This tended to be a more complicated way to fix the hair, but soon the writing was on the wall. Wearing the covering to school became expected, especially by those who were considered spiritual. And so, my eldest daughter changed her hairstyle and began to wear her head covering on an every day basis. After all, women were to cover their heads for prayer, and the need to pray could come at any time.

A second situation came when the P.E. classes began to have swimming as part of their curriculum. She came home and said she needed a note to excuse her from swimming "for religious reasons." We were surprised, and asked, "Don't the girls swim by themselves, and also the boys? As long as it's segregated swimming, what is the problem?" We had always been a family who swam, either in our backyard in an above ground pool or in the river nearby, but now she was not supposed to swim?

She explained it to us, "Mom, if I swim, the other Mennonite girls will not want me to be part of their group—they might not even talk to me, so please, write the note for me." And so we did, all the while wondering why some of the decisions we were expected to make seemed so challenging to us. We found ourselves complying but not being happy about it. We wanted our children to have a positive school experience and not be outcasts from some of their peers, and it seemed they could not always be friends with both their Holdeman and their non-Holdeman classmates. This division was not something I experienced during my school years, although my husband remembers this separation between Holdemans and other school kids as being a normal pattern while in school in Kansas. This was particularly true during World War II when it was known that Holdemans did not serve in the military because of their non-resistant stand. This "unpatriotic" response to the war was certainly frowned on and even ridiculed by some of the town folks, and this attitude filtered down to their children who took it upon themselves to taunt their Holdeman classmates.

Our children had friends both in and out of the church. However, if we as parents were also friends with their friends' parents and connected socially, their friendship would extend to both school and church, adding that duel dimension. For my husband and me, as with most Holdeman couples, our social interaction was limited entirely to church families. This tended to make our church lives and our children's school lives quite different, but children are resilient and learned to bounce from one mode to the other quite easily. Sundays were times to get dressed up, get the entire family into the car, remembering to bring our S.S. books with us, and off we'd go, to Sunday School first, and then to the church service that followed immediately. At church the older children would sit quietly with their friends while the youngest ones were cared for by Mom and Dad, each on their separate sides of the auditorium, during the service. Most services went from 10:45 to 12 o'clock, and when little ones got restless, we did not allow them to disrupt the service but would take them to the baby room, one on the men's side and one on the women's side. This was a place to change diapers, put little ones down in the cribs provided, or just entertain them quietly in some way.

After the service, we would frequently invite other families over for Sunday dinner or be invited out to their homes. Usually there would be a roast of some sort baking in the oven, and the lady of the house gladly accepted the offered help by any female guests to get the "feast" on the table. We would all be seated around the table, unless there were more children than could fit at the adult table, and these children might have a plate fixed for them and eat at another table somewhere. After a time of visiting and sometimes singing together, the visitors would go home and take a rest before evening service, which started at seven p.m. and would last until about nine. By this time we were ready to go home, put the children to bed, and fall into bed ourselves. After all, tomorrow would be a school day. We were very comfortable in this routine, the same one our parents had raised us with, and we were not looking for change.

SO MANY QUESTIONS

Chapter Fourteen

I was cooking supper one night when a friend stopped by for a chat. We had become friends because she, a Holdeman, had achieved the distinction of being a credentialed teacher and still retained her membership. Of course, there were special circumstances. She had taught school without a credential at the Navaho Mission the church had established in Arizona, but when she was pressured by the state to get her credential, she had been able, with church approval, to attend college. While it was acceptable, with permission from the ministry, to attend college to get a nursing degree, teaching was not in the same category. The church sponsored a few nursing homes and hospitals but no schools.

I was glad to see her because I had been struggling with a revelation I didn't know what to do with. I can no longer remember what the issue was, but I burst out with what I thought was a bomb shell—"Inez, what do you do when you realize you no longer believe everything the church teaches?" I was stunned with this dilemma—I had always been honest with my faith, and now I had the biggest challenge of my personal integrity; how could I pretend to believe something I didn't!

My friend chuckled and replied that it was no big deal! And to her, it wasn't. She said, "We all come to that point, sooner or later, and you have to weigh the advantages and disadvantages. We are part of a warm, loving, supportive church that will stand by us in trouble and care about us like family. On the other hand, it's a cold world out there, and it would be a very lonely transition to try to adjust to something completely unfamiliar. There are some things you just don't talk about."

I listened, and we talked more, but it was not a satisfying answer to me. Just keep it to myself? Just sit on it? How in the world was I going to be able to do that! I had no idea how many questions would come up as we dealt with issues regarding our children's assimilation into public school. Many questions were still ahead!

Since our children went to public school, the school bus came around seven-thirty a.m. to pick them up, so weekday mornings had to move quickly. There was a time when we had five children of various school ages, so getting them ready and often packing each one a lunch was a challenge. Fortunately, our children enjoyed school and were willing and eager to go. As a mom, I had the yearly parent-teacher conference, which I never minded since our children always had a good report. They knew how to behave and do their school work and tended to be in the upper level of the class. It was truly rewarding to listen to the teachers brag on our children. Willis, of course, was always working for a business in a neighboring town to provide for this rather large family and was never privileged to meet with the teachers. That was considered the mother's prerogative.

While sports are so much a part of children's lives today, our children could take P.E. but could not be engaged in after-school sports. This would have involved bringing them from our country home into town and to the athletic fields, but we likely would have provided transportation had after-school sports been allowed. Again, this was a generally-held concept, not a clearly defined church rule. Many years later, our youngest son would become a track star, but by this time we were no longer members of the church. He would have privileges our older kids did not have, as would our youngest daughter, who in junior high was able to participate in the school band. None of the older children had the opportunity to be involved in music instruction.

I went to visit a favorite cousin one day and we talked about the challenges of raising our children and trying to toe the line in every interaction with "the world." As I was preparing to leave, one of us said, "Wouldn't it be nice if we could meet with a small group in a home Bible study and look at some of these issues from a Biblical standpoint?" Of course! That seemed like a good solution, and because one of the ministers in our congregation was about my age and a cousin of mine, we decided to invite him and his wife for that purpose so that we three couples could have a relaxed, informal discussion. And this is what we did. In the beginning our talks were pleasant and conversational. I suspect we withheld our most troubling questions. However, for the third gathering I had invited another couple to join us, and that evening turned out differently. As we sat around the dining room table, I decided to ask a question about the devotional covering. My question was, "If it is so important that we cover our heads with a little black cap that sits more on the back of our heads than a real 'head covering,' why did I not feel a sense of truly pleasing God by this practice? I was willing to wear it—it had become second nature after many years of wearing one, but somehow I wanted to see it as a blessing and to feel that I was truly honoring God."

That was discussed, and I believe the answer was that our obedience to God's commands didn't always give us some kind of affirmation, but that we needed to be obedient anyway. But it was the new couple who really turned our meeting on its head—the husband opened the floodgates to a very emotional conversation. He told how that he had been the "proverbial good boy" while at home, and had thought he was doing the right things, living in obedience to the church and his parents, and that all was well in his Christian walk. But then he went away to "voluntary service," the alternative to military service for conscientious objectors, and to his alarm he found he was filled with uncertainties and questions. He realized that he wasn't really sure where he stood with the Lord or whether he was truly pleasing God or just jumping through the hoops that our church expected. He told our little group that evening about how he had walked the streets at night in the large city in which he was stationed, crying out to God in prayer and feeling like he had few answers for his many questions. He felt confused in that, having done all that was expected of him by the church and his parents, he had no real confidence that he was pleasing God. He felt unsure of God's plan for his life. His testimony implied that the church he had placed his faith in was probably not preparing their young people to go out into the outside world with confidence. Even though our church had established what they called a "preparatory class" to prepare our young men for challenges they might meet in the world away from their familiar farming communities, it was inadequate preparation.

These two testimonies were very disconcerting to our minister and his wife. It seemed our minister had two people on his hands whose attitudes were not completely supportive of the teachings of the church: One had dared to question the devotional covering, a fundamental doctrine of the church, while the other who, having followed all the church rules, did not seem confident that all was well. It seemed he lacked the assurance that his life was pleasing to God and that the church doctrines he'd been taught were sufficient to make him the Godly man that God wanted him to be.

This turn of events was very challenging to our minister; he had been expecting to be able to answer a few simple questions to a group of church members who would simply respond, "Oh, thanks—that helps us understand things better." Instead we seemed to be questioning basic doctrines, and that was not okay. Finally, he stood up, threw his hands up in the air, and said, "I give up," meaning, apparently, that if we did not have faith to receive the truth as he presented it, he could not help us.

As the hostess of the evening, I was alarmed. I did not want anyone to leave our home having had a "bad experience" and feeling that they had been attacked or misunderstood. Surely prayer would resolve the problem. And so I asked, "Would it be alright if we stood up around the table, held hands and prayed that we might all be forgiving and understanding, that no one would be hurt?"

This seemed to be a good solution, or so I thought. Surely asking questions and seeking answers should not be such a radical idea that it would divide us as members of the same church body. There had been no intent to cause problems or be antagonistic in any way. We had simply been honest with the questions that were on our hearts.

However, as we later learned, the prayer did not calm the waters as we had hoped. Our minister felt obligated to go to the staff of our local church and report on our Bible study. We heard later than he had stated that "Willis and Leona, and perhaps others in the group, are not as stable as was thought—it appears they doubt some of the essential doctrines of the faith." At the next church council meeting, one of the ministers spoke to the issue by saying that asking questions about basic doctrines, such as the woman's prayer covering, was evidence of not truly being grounded in the faith—that it was important to accept all of the major doctrinal points by faith and without question. Understanding why was not important. We knew that our desire to become stronger in the faith was the purpose of our Bible study, but somehow instead of getting the help we needed, we were now judged to be unstable.

By the close of that council meeting at our church, I felt singled out for the first time in my life. We had friends somewhat older than us who lived right across the church yard, and my husband and I walked over immediately after the meeting to talk with them. By this time, I was in tears, and they put their arms around us and comforted us, telling us that we should not take this so personally—that it would blow over and, in the meantime, it would be wise to just back off a bit. Good advice, we thought. Asking questions obviously only brought trouble to the one who was questioning. But we did know we could bring our uncertainties to the Lord, and this we did. We spent more time reading the Word and praying, knowing that God had the answers to any questions we might have. I remember praying, "Lord, we thought we were doing things right—that we were going to our spiritual leaders for answers to our questions, and all we've done is get ourselves in trouble. Please, Father, help us find answers by your Holy Spirit and not be the cause of trouble to our church leaders." We were confident God not only knew the answers to our questions but that we could trust Him to enlighten us. We never doubted God. We knew He was always faithful and He was not confused.

We have no idea whether we, my husband and I, had more questions than our friends and relatives in the church or just why we felt such a strong need to understand the doctrines of the church and to live them out in obedience. We assumed that every rule or regulation was based on Scripture, and that if we only understood the Scriptural basis more clearly, we could be stronger in our faith, particularly as we handed it down to our children. And while we supposed there was some variance between believers in the way we lived out our faith, we did not think there would be major differences in understanding.

During earlier years, I had attempted to read the writings of John Holdeman, our church founder, but that had generally brought only confusion. His thoughts and ideas were often hidden in language that was muddled and unclear, and I would find myself giving up—again. Then too, while we honored Holdeman as the founder of our denomination, we were aware that it was God and His Bible in which we placed our ultimate trust. We also assumed that our faithful attendance to all church services, both morning and evening preaching services and Wednesday night Bible studies, would be the on-going source of our growth in spiritual knowledge and understanding. And that was our ultimate desire—to live out Scripture in the day and age in which we lived, just as earlier Christians had lived out their faith in their time. We wanted to be true believers. That was the calling we felt upon our lives.

This was our state of mind as we stopped our home Bible study and decided to simply wait on the Lord. There were no major issues that we struggled with on a daily basis. We continued to conduct our lives as we always had, following the teachings of our church, attending church services regularly, socializing with our church friends, trying to be good parents to our six children, but being careful now not to rock the boat. But when and how God answered our prayers we simply knew, without a shadow of a doubt, that He had something planned for us that we had not anticipated. The question was, could we rise to the challenge? Would we be able to obediently follow Jesus wherever He led? Could our trust in Him be so complete that it would take precedence over the traditions we had grown up with? Could we break the chains of legalism that had kept us bound for so many years?

PHOTOS

Leona's grandparents, Ben C. and Suzanna Koehn

Leona's parents, Alfred and Anna Koehn

Leona, age 4

Willis, age 6

Leona, early teens

Willis, early teens

Willis and Leona, early 1970's

Willis and Leona 1975

Willis and Leona, 25th wedding anniversary, 1977

Willis and Leona, Christmas in the 1980's

Family Christmas 1970's

Mother's Day 1970's

Willis and boys snow tubing 1970's

Micki

Bruce

Bethany

Danny

Darlisa

Jon

Leona's father, Alfred Koehn, 1990's

Willis and Leona at Bass Lake, 2002

Willis and Leona, 50th wedding anniversary, 2002

Grandkids skit, 1990's

Grandkids at family BBQ, 2002

Grandkids in pool, 2002

Grandkids with grandparents at beach, 2008

Grandkids Christmas 2010

Family Christmas 2010

OTHER LOVES ALL FLEE

continued—Part Two

AN ENCOUNTER
WITH JESUS

Chapter Fifteen

As I consider the second part of this testimony, I proceed with trepidation because what is precious to us tends to be greeted with skepticism by others. Isaiah said it like this in the 53rd chapter: "Who has believed our report, and to whom is the arm of the Lord revealed? "He then prophesies about the coming Messiah, but it is the "suffering Savior" he presents, not the military leader the Jews were looking for, and therefore they neither understood nor did they believe Isaiah's report.

Obviously, many people who have heard "our report" did not believe God had spoken but rather that we had been beguiled by the Evil One. And since the Scripture teaches that we are to test the spirits, caution is important for each of us.

Admittedly, deception is lurking behind many decisions built on good intentions. However, as we continued in prayer and with much searching of the Word of God, we could not deny that God was speaking. The question was, would we listen at the cost of losing something precious to us, our church family? Could it be possible that what we had been taught was "the one true visible church" was, in fact simply a denomination that had elevated itself to that status? Could it be that the church Jesus was coming back to claim as His bride would include all born again believers who had come to the cross with their sins and been forgiven? Were they Christ followers even if they didn't look like us?

I also know that personal experiences are suspect, simply because they ARE personal and are not experienced by everyone in the same way. One must weigh them carefully because they may be interpreted with much of the individual's own thoughts and ideas creeping in and distorting the message. I think of Saul/Paul's experience of being stopped in his tracks by Jesus on the Damascus Road; it is obvious his fellow Pharisees did not see this as an act of God. Very likely they had another explanation, possibly an experience of "sunstroke" or even deception, something of that nature when he reported being struck down by a "bright light." Surely Saul had friends among the Pharisees with whom he was eager to share his encounter with God, but I suspect there was nothing Saul could say to convince them that it was actually God who had spoken. Saul's experience was a supernatural event, life-changing in its implications, turning him in an entirely different direction. As you know from the account, Saul was shocked by Jesus' question, "Saul, Saul, why do you persecute me?" Why indeed? He sincerely believed he was doing God's work in rounding up Christians. Now the unexpected had happened and he could not deny it nor could he turn back.

So many things start with a phone call. In May of '72, we had some friends who called to tell us they had had an unsettling conversation with some of their friends from the congregation in Glenn, Ca, the Holdeman community in Northern California. These friends had come to our locality because of their seriously ill father whose life was in the balance, and had met with our friends, an unusual meeting, as it turned out. They seemed to be filled with a joy in Jesus that was different than our friends had seen or heard before, and they were excited about answered prayers they had experienced. This conversation between the two couples raised questions in the minds of the couple who lived in our community regarding the Christian faith and how it was lived it out in the Holdeman church. Listening to them talk about this conversation on the phone, we thought it sounded like a good discussion waiting to happen. Why not invite them over, as well as several other young couples, to join in an evening of fellowship? We ended up with five couples besides ourselves who were able to come to our home that evening. Most were in their twenties and were without children, while we were in our late thirties and had six, the youngest of which was two and a half. I suppose I prepared dessert, thinking we'd have a fun time around the table, talking seriously, of course, but also laughing and joking.

Our guests came and we settled in the living room, sending our children to play in their rooms, and very quickly we noticed a different attitude in the couple who had come from the North. It seemed they wanted to talk mostly about Jesus and how they were now experiencing Him in a very personal way. Also, they were eager to tell us about some answers to prayers that had amazed them. We were quite taken aback—that is, this was not the usual kind of conversation we generally had when we got together as Holdeman couples. The husband who had called to ask if they could come and examine some issues that seemed controversial considering our church teachings, asked several questions about various Scriptures and how we felt about them. Our conversation seemed to focus on how real Jesus actually was to us in our everyday lives. Also, there were questions about how Scripture should be lived out in the times in which we lived. This was definitely a spiritual direction we did not take in our usual gatherings, and after a time of questions, one of the guests from a distance suggested that we have a time of prayer in which anyone who wanted to could pray, or not, according to their own wishes. Somewhat reluctantly we complied with his suggestion. At his request, we stood in our living room making two large circles, the ladies in the center circle, the gentlemen on the outside. As the hostess I remember thinking that this was going nowhere, that people would not be open to praying in this manner, and since women particularly were not accustomed to praying in groups, it just was not going to happen.

Imagine my surprise when, starting with the gentleman who had suggested it, a most beautiful prayer time followed. Several of the men prayed, followed by several of the women, and as the prayers intensified, a few individuals prayed repeatedly and with profound feeling. Most prayers were centered on their own needs and their own desire for a stronger relationship with Jesus. They seemed to be cries from the heart, lifted to God and expressing their request for a closer walk with Him. Often they included the question, "Are the attitudes of my heart and the actions of my life acceptable to you, my Lord and Savior? Please help me to know if I am honoring you by the decisions I make and the way I live my life." It seemed evident that Jesus was guiding and leading us into a search for a deeper walk with Him, and I'm quite sure that we were all surprised by what was happening. This must have gone on for thirty to forty minutes, and when we stopped we knew God had met with us and was moving on our hearts to seek a closer relationship with

Him. For this particular group of Holdeman Mennonites, the evening had taken an unexpected turn.

When we finished praying, our friend asked if there was anyone who wanted personal prayer, and my husband, thinking they would take his request with them and pray at home, said, "Yes, I struggle with doubts and questions that I don't have answers for." To his surprise, he was asked to sit on a chair while several men "laid hands on him" and prayed for him right there on the spot. After this a few others asked for personal prayer. My eldest daughter, having just home from youth meeting, stood in the doorway watching, and when she was asked if she wanted prayer, she replied, "I don't know—I just want what you have." Soon she was sitting in a chair while several people "laid hands" on her shoulders and prayed that her walk with the Lord would be genuine and meaningful. After the prayer, she left the room in order to help the little ones in our family get ready for bed. For my husband and me, the intensity of our prayer time had so absorbed our thoughts we had paid no attention to getting our children to bed; later we learned that our two older children had taken care of that responsibility. Being a school night, our lack of concern over bedtimes was in itself unusual.

By this time, it was after eleven o'clock, and people began saying their goodbyes and heading out to their cars. My husband saw the last couple out while I waited in the living room, hoping to discuss with him what had happened that night. When he had locked the door and turned out the yard light, he came into the room where I was waiting. We put our arms around each other, intending to pray together once more before going to bed. I cannot remember if we actually began praying when we became aware that something very unusual was happening, and soon we stood in silence as God invaded our lives with an outpouring of love such as we had never experienced or even known was possible. It was such a "holy moment," and it would change us forever. From this point on our lives would be divided between "before" and "after" that incredible time with the Lord.

How does one explain the unexplainable? I see the same stumbling of words in the New Testament account when Jesus' disciples attempted to describe what happened on what we call "The Mount of Transfiguration." We all know how to talk about the usual routines of our lives, but when God shows up, we stumble for words. As my husband and I stood with our arms around each other, we both were conscious that we stood in the Presence of Jesus. We didn't see Him, but He seemed to be standing just a few feet away, and we felt such awe. Both of us became aware that He was pouring out His love, over us and into our hearts in such a powerful way that we could hardly take it in. It was so intense that at first we could not speak, but finally I asked my husband, "Do you feel what I feel?" and my husband, who tends to downplay things, said, "Oh, yes, Honey—isn't it wonderful!" We did not know it was possible to experience such a warm and loving Presence as we felt in those moments of time. It seemed this outpouring of love went on for several minutes, or even longer, as time became insignificant. Even now we do not have words to describe the intensity of love that poured over us and into our hearts, bathing us with an awareness of the all-encompassing love of Jesus. We were filled with the joy of His Presence in a way we'd never imagined possible.

Then, as we stood in silence, the Holy Spirit began to heal hurts and answer questions we'd had that we struggled with, responding to our individual needs with such tenderness and comfort. For my husband, having lost his own mother at age two, there had always been an empty place deep inside that Jesus now began to fill with His love. Not only did he heal the pain that growing up without his own mother had brought, He also poured out His love over the hurts he'd received and the loneliness he'd experienced as a child in his large family of origin. His step-mother had her hands full with tasks of cooking, washing, and cleaning for this family that with "his, hers, and theirs" eventually numbered fifteen children. Life had not been easy, and as a child he had felt lonely and little more than a burden to his family. He had often survived by fading into the background and trying to slip by unnoticed. He felt he was unimportant.

I, on the other hand, as a mother of six, often felt inadequate in being the mother I felt called to be—there simply was not enough time or energy to spread out between my six precious children and the time commitments it takes to raise a family of that size. I heard the Lord saying to my heart, "Leona, if you will give me your day, I will direct your time, and what you don't get done that day, I never intended you to do. Do not feel guilty." A huge burden rolled off my back as I realized that Jesus had just taken my inadequacy on Himself, and that as I obeyed Him, I could truly be free of guilt. He would guide me in

His plan for me and my remorse over unfinished tasks was not a result of disapproval from Jesus. I was set free.

Neither of us remembers how long we stood in silence as the healing love of Jesus poured into and over our hearts, and the emotions we felt were almost more than we could take in. Finally, we came to a place where we began, very gingerly, to speak the words, "Thank You, Jesus— Thank You so very, very much for Your love that is so much more than we could ever have imagined." Our hearts were filled with awe and wonder over His grace and mercy toward us, and we both knew our lives were forever changed.

As the intensity of that experience lessened and we remembered we needed to go to bed and to sleep, I knew one thing for sure: I could not live without this deep and holy awareness of Jesus in my life. I remember praying, "Lord, if you're not there in the morning, I don't want to wake up." Then, after replaying this experience in my mind for some time, I fell asleep.

My husband, on the other hand, apparently could not sleep at all, and after some time had passed, he got up, got dressed, and walked outside on the driveways through our almond orchards, raising his hands and praising God. We did not know that people of our generation ever did this—we had never seen it done, but my husband was so filled with the love of Jesus that he couldn't help himself. The intensity of praise within his heart simply had to be expressed. Knowing how reserved his natural temperament is, this was a most unlikely thing for him to do. He did eventually come to bed, but he knew he wanted to visit his step-mom the next day.

Rediscovering the Word

Chapter Sixteen

We got up the next morning to total peace in our household. My eldest daughter, getting ready for school, came into the kitchen and said to her father, "Oh, Daddy, isn't it wonderful!" It seemed the peace that passes understanding just permeated our house that morning. Five of our six children were in school, the youngest in kindergarten and the two eldest in high school, so after breakfast and getting them out to the bus stop, my husband and I sat down on our sofa and opened the Bible. I am not sure why we opened to the Book of Acts, but as we began to read, the Word of God came alive. We would read aloud together, but periodically we would stop and say, "Oh my, did you know it said that?" This was strange since we both had grown up with regular Bible reading in our individual families and were always in church where the Word of God was read and expounded. We were totally amazed as we saw how the Lord had made Himself so real to the early church through the power of the Holy Spirit. It is no wonder their lives were "turned upside down", the phrase Luke uses to explain what had happened. We also understood their desire to gather daily, break bread together, and praise God for His love. For us also, prayer had become the most desired activity we could possibly engage in. We had not yet heard the term, "conversational prayer," but we had found that talking to God as to a friend was immensely satisfying, and we were drawn to frequent prayer as we went through our day.

We spent most of that first morning rediscovering the truths of the Bible, the same Bible that we had known all our lives but now was speaking directly to us and with great clarity. The truth was, the Word thrilled us and nourished our hearts as never before—it seemed to be fresh and new and so focused on Jesus and His redeeming love.

However, this love wasn't given to make us simply feel good, but rather was a call for action. Later that day, Willis went to visit his step-mom for one purpose only, to ask her forgiveness for his part in the family dissension while still at home. He remembered discussions that had not been kind but had often been intensely critical. He also told her he loved her, which he had never said before and certainly had never felt until this time. She did not respond with an affirmation of her love, probably because they did not talk that openly about loving one another in their family. It would take years before Willis would hear her say those words.

I remember opening my sewing machine and propping a song book up so that as I sewed I also sang. There was one song in which the chorus repeated, "Praise the Lord, praise the Lord, let the earth hear His voice," which I sang over and over again. I knew many wonderful hymns, but this day I wanted to sing hymns of praise to my Savior, the One who had filled me with such overflowing love. I also remember how when Willis and I met out in the yard or wherever, we would put our arms around each other and pray prayers of joy and thanksgiving. It was a wonderful time as we basked in the fullness of His love.

As excited as we were about finding the "answer" to every challenge in our lives, we also thought of various friends who were struggling in one way or another. We couldn't wait to share that Jesus had shown Himself to us as the answer to every situation anyone could face. In fact, the very next day, the husband of a recent acquaintance of mine, not a Holdeman, called to tell me that his wife, who had just become a first-time-mother, was having problems. Apparently, as he said, she had "lost her mind and was being totally unreasonable," and he was afraid that she might harm their baby. He asked if I could come to their home and help her to calm down. I was amazed and somewhat puzzled. This was a new friend, someone I didn't know well, but I immediately recognized that this opportunity was one God had specifically designed for me to share His love, so I said, "Yes, I will come."

I drove into town and she met me at her door. Her words were "If you don't want to be involved in our marital troubles, don't even come in."

I said, "Please, let me tell you what God has done in our home, and perhaps it will help."

So we sat down together and the first thing that came out of my mouth was, "You know, it isn't your husband who is the problem—it is Satan, the evil one who wants to destroy our homes and our families. Your husband is not a bad person—the fact that two people who love each other are now fighting is exactly what Satan attempts to bring about in every home, but you don't have to let him. He is a divider who stirs up trouble wherever he can, but Jesus wants to pour His love into your hearts. Will you let him?"

She responded with, "Satan! Oh, my! I learned about him in catechism, but I've forgotten about him since then."

"Unfortunately, he hasn't forgotten you," I said, "and he is a trouble-maker from the beginning. He will do everything he can to destroy your home or any home, for that matter."

I asked if she had a Bible, and she said she had a big one somewhere, but since she was uncertain as to where it was, it seemed more convenient to just share Scripture from my heart and to pray with her. We prayed that God would protect this precious family from the wiles of Satan and that Jesus would change her husband while at work so that he would come home and be the helpful man he usually was.

Very early the next morning, my phone rang, and it was my friend of the day before. She was so excited as she told me, "You'll never believe this—my husband came home a different man. He's been so understanding and just as helpful as could be, and we are enjoying our baby together."

I chuckled and said, "I'm not surprised—we prayed, you know, and Jesus is so eager to restore the family. Call me anytime, please. We can talk about what Jesus has in mind for our lives as we live joyfully together within our families."

This is only one example of several opportunities we had to share the incredible love Jesus has for those who seek Him. We also knew of a Holdeman family who was struggling with relationship problems for which there seemed no solution. How we longed to share with them the joy we had found in putting Jesus first, and how powerful the simple prayer of faith could be to change situations.

FINDING OURSELVES
IN HOT WATER

Chapter Seventeen

However, the response toward us was very different with our Holdeman church family. One of the wives, who along with her husband had been at our home the previous evening, went directly to her parents the next morning to give her mom an account of the visit-turned-prayer meeting. Her mother was alarmed at her report of unsupervised prayer by a group of lay people, and told her she needed to go talk to the church ministers immediately. In a day or two our senior pastor called to ask if he could visit us.

We were not anticipating any kind of trouble—in fact, we were thrilled that Jesus was now real and alive in our hearts, and we looked forward to sharing the account of His amazing outpouring of love with our minister. However, he came into our home, his face very grave, and asked us to tell him in detail what had transpired at our house that particular evening. He listened soberly.

In our eagerness to share the reality of Jesus' love that we had experienced, we told him everything that had happened, that as the evening progressed we had begun to sense the presence of Jesus and the strengthening of our faith. However, it was the prayer time he was most concerned about. We explained how we had been led to pray, standing in a circle and inviting anyone who wanted to pray to do so, bringing their requests to the Lord. We told him how surprised we were that our guests were willing to open up and participate, an unexpected response from the young couples, especially the women. Of course women prayed, but usually only silently, or with their children at bedtime or perhaps when saying grace at the table while the husband was away. However, it was what happened afterwards with my husband and me that we were most excited about and wanted to share. It seemed our words were completely inadequate in explaining how precious the experience had been and how it had changed our lives.

Our pastor listened, saying very little, mostly just questioning the process or style of prayer that we had used. He mentioned that it was not necessary for more than **one** person to pray—that would have been enough, and would have been in accord with our usual custom. It was common practice in our parents and grandparents' day to have evening devotions before guests went home. Both my husband and I had grown up with this familiar tradition, but now it appeared we had stepped over the line.

In a matter of a couple of days, our second minister came to our home, and we repeated the same story. Our third minister was seriously ill at the time and was bedfast, so we went to his house to tell him what had happened. We were still of the mind that the outpouring of love we had received was God's gracious gift to us and that it was available to all. It could be received by anyone willing to pray with an honest heart, believing that God would answer None of the three ministers responded with an admonition or any kind of suggestion that we may have overstepped—in fact, they hardly responded at all. They listened, then thanked us and left.

Soon we heard by the grapevine that all was not well, and that we would be called into account for "an irregular" visit/prayer time. By the time the members meeting was called, gossip had run rampant and all sorts of insinuations had arisen. Of course, we were willing to explain what had happened in our home to anyone and everyone, but we were never given that opportunity. A council meeting was called, and we were shocked when one of the ministers at the meeting got up and announced, "Brethren, Satan has invaded our congregation and we must rout him out." How had it gotten from a desire in the hearts of several young couples to draw nearer to the Lord to instead be the work of Satan? And how had prayer become "an act of Satan?"

After a time of discussion, primarily by the ministers while the congregation listened, my father, a well-respected ordained deacon in the church, slowly got up and said, "I don't know if my children did everything right that night, I wasn't there. But I do know they have a new love for God and a hunger for His Word." Then he sat down. Sensing the turn of events and where this might possibly be going, I thought, "Oh dear, I hope this doesn't get him in trouble." But it did.

Eventually he and his wife would be disciplined also, the primary charge being that he had dared, as an ordained man, to cause division among the ministry. We went home that night, saddened by what we still thought was a misunderstanding, that what was such a blessing to us was turning out to be a real obstacle for our beloved brethren.

Surprising things transpired in the following weeks. Our church friends seemed to withdraw, and since we didn't want them to also be disciplined, we respected their fear. One family, who had been at our home before the members meeting occurred and knew nothing about our visit/prayer meeting with other friends, did a complete turn around. Before the council meeting when they had visited us we had talked about the Lord and sung a few hymns and had a prayer together. Then, as they stood in our doorway saying goodbye, the wife said, with tears in her eyes, "We have never enjoyed an evening as much as this one." However, after our unplanned prayer meeting was exposed at the members meeting at church she met me on the church yard and said, "I'm sorry we had such a good time at your house—we shouldn't have." There was really no way I could respond to her statement with anything more than, "I'm so sorry you feel that way."

VENTURING OUT

Chapter Eighteen

Our newfound love for Jesus in our home and in our daily lives inspired us to seek out fellowship with others who loved Jesus and wanted to pray and worship Him in their homes. I cannot remember how we first began to hear of prayer meetings and Bible studies here and there, but somehow we did. We knew that Holdemans usually did not fellowship with believers outside their own church. However, we were desperate to connect with those who might understand and share our excitement in learning to know this Jesus whose love was so personal and who heard and answered prayers. Our hunger for fellowship with like-minded people moved us to respond to invitations outside our own church. That was obviously crossing the line because we knew we were not even to think of non-Holdemans as believers since they were not baptized members in our own church.

In spite of that knowledge, for a time we became quite regular attenders at a prayer meeting held in a neighboring town. This group of people came from a variety of church backgrounds, the identity of which seemed to be unimportant to those who gathered together to pray. We were new to the idea that a group of people would come together in a home, not to eat or to play games, but simply to pray. They prayed with a firm conviction that God would not only hear but would answer their prayers, sometimes in unexpected ways.

One evening as we stood in a circle praying, one of the leaders of the prayer group walked over to the wife of a couple we had brought with us, and in a quiet voice, he made a startling announcement. He shared with my friend, "The baby you are carrying is normal and healthy, and the Lord does not want you to abort this child."

You can imagine the shock, since none of us even knew she was pregnant. As soon as we got back into the car, she said to me, "Why did you tell him I was pregnant!"

I replied that I had no idea she was expecting a child, nor did I realize the quandary she was in. Because her husband had been addicted to pain medication, and because of the stress in their home, she had supposed her pregnancy could not possibly produce a normal child and she was considering her options. They already had two sons and weren't really planning on more children. In this particular case the answer to prayer was probably life-saving, and what a joy when the birth several months later produced a normal, healthy baby girl. For us it was evidence that God's desire to reveal His truth to His people was very personal and clear. When I see her today and know that she and her husband are Bible-believing Christians, I remember that there was a time when her life was at risk, and I praise God for the discernment of Godly believers.

In spite of these connections with other believers now and then, Willis and I had every intention to remain in the church of our childhood, but the hunger in our hearts to share this love with others compelled us to seek out homes where people gathered to pray. It seemed odd to have to meet for prayer and fellowship on the sly with other believers, but the wall of rejection built by our own people was so high we could not scale it. As much as we wanted to share our newfound joy in Jesus with them, we could find no way to do so. However, we were open for any opportunities that might come our way with our own people, and we never missed a church service at our local congregation, nor did we or our children ever miss Sunday school. Some of our own people were so afraid of us they would literally turn their backs as we walked up to a group, or give us a superficial greeting and smile, then walk away. We found ourselves very lonely among the people we had known all of our lives and had socialized with up to that point.

We really broke tradition when we attended a revival meeting in a church in Modesto that was not of our own denomination. It was here that our second daughter responded to the call of God on her life and gave her heart to Jesus. We were so excited and thrilled by her new birth, but found ourselves in the difficult position of not being able to tell anyone. To "get saved" in the wrong church was worse than not getting saved at all, it seemed, so we kept it to ourselves, not telling our own people. Our daughter, however, shared with a few school friends, which would lead to her being ostracized at school by her friends who attended our church. Interestingly enough, she did make a new friend with whom she would share Bible reading time and enjoy having times of fellowship. Still, she missed the camaraderie with her old friends.

In the fall, our usual process of revival meetings was scheduled to occur in our home church. Revivals were traditionally a two-week long series of meetings held nightly for the purpose of encouraging the faithful and also convicting the disobedient and leading them back to obedient living. During the second week of meetings, the messages are especially focused on inviting the unsaved, which would usually be children of church people who had not yet received the Lord personally. Occasionally an "outsider" might be interested in the Gospel and the life of simplicity required by those who adopt this culture. There are a small number of people of non-Holdeman backgrounds, who, upon hearing the preaching in a Holdeman church or in observing the simplicity of this lifestyle, are drawn to this group. If they desire to also become members, they would then need to be converted and baptized into the fold.

During revivals it is the custom for entire families to attend night after night to listen to the preaching of the Word. We were among this number, hoping to demonstrate our concern for our own lives and to reconnect with our loved ones in our own church. When, after a week of meetings it became time to call a "members' meeting," we knew our situation would be discussed. Before the meeting, Willis and I made the decision to do whatever was asked of us, regardless of how we felt personally. When a vote was taken regarding whether those present felt that this unknown spirit troubling certain members of the church was a "sectarian spirit" and should be stamped out, we too arose to our feet. We had been told that if we went against our personal feelings and were obedient to the ministers, God would change our hearts somehow and we would again be in fellowship. That sounded good and worth trying, even though it seemed a rather strange doctrine.

I will always remember how it felt to stand up and vote against ourselves. We did what we were told to do, but after church was dismissed, we fled to our car and quickly went home. There, I fell on my face on the kitchen floor, pleading with God to forgive us for attempting to please our brethren while denying this Jesus who loved us with unfailing love. My husband joined me in this prayer of contrition. We prayed together for some time as a couple, asking for forgiveness. We knew exactly how the apostle Peter felt when he denied Christ and then heard the rooster crow, just as Jesus had forewarned. By the time peace again came to our hearts, we knew one thing—we would never again deny the Lord and His leading in our lives. It was during those meetings that we were officially placed "on repentance," by the brotherhood, the step before excommunication.

Being placed "on repentance" is a church decision made by the membership when the local church body formally asks a disobedient member to repent and "show fruits of repentance." We were now publicly identified as members who had willfully fallen into sin. Before this charge could be lifted we would need to show evidence that we had turned away from our waywardness and were now faithfully following the path required by the church. Interestingly enough, there were no church rules that we had actually broken, so the call to repentance was a bit vague. We had, however, visited with other "so-called Christians" and prayed with them in non-Mennonite homes. This is a serious charge because it would imply that there are other believers in the community who were not part of "the one true visible church." It is called "spiritual adultery," and is probably the most serious charge of all, worse than such things as going to movies, owning a camera, taking pictures, or listening to the radio. These lesser sins had all been a part of my husband's past while living as a church member in his childhood home, a minister's home, but he had slid under the radar and had never been disciplined for these misdeeds. Fellowshipping with other believers was far more serious, and we were asked to stop attending outside prayer meetings immediately.

Connecting with Our Hippie Friends

Chapter Nineteen

The Holdeman Mennonite church, officially called The Church of God in Christ (Mennonite), is an exclusivist group that interacts socially only within their own group. Of course they are friendly with surrounding neighbors and fellow workers they might meet on a job, and they will go out of their way to help needy individuals who come to them for help. They also participate in a larger Mennonite group called Mennonite Union Aid, (MUA), a relief organization which addresses needs around the world. They have a strong commitment to serve as a "Good Samaritan" in any situation of need, particularly when natural disasters occur and clean-up help is needed. Reaching out to help with caring, responsible workers who supply whatever help is needed when a tragedy has occurred is one of their strengths. However, their teaching of finding fellowship only with their own is deeply ingrained. Few Holdemans know their non-Holdeman neighbors well nor would they be inclined to interact socially in such ways as visiting in their homes. They certainly would not consider visiting their churches or any kind of spiritual fellowship meetings in their homes. Keeping oneself "unspotted from the world" is a doctrine strongly held and practiced. Being "too friendly" with non-members, those who do not share the same church doctrine, is not only discouraged but might call for reproof or even church action against such a member.

Because of this teaching, our family had never become close with any community residents who might be "so-called Christians" but were not in our church. Therefore, because our church friends were now afraid to associate with us, we spent much time alone. This loneliness contributed to why we were eager to attend Bible studies or prayer meetings in various homes in the community. Though sponsored by other Christians, not Holdemans, we found in them the same desire to grow closer to Jesus in their hearts as in ours. They did not dress in the prescribed fashion we had been taught, but they had the same hunger in their hearts.

This was during the 1970's, a time when there seemed to be a move of God throughout the country simply called "The Jesus Movement." This move of God was causing unlikely people to find the Lord and there were small groups springing up in many places for the purpose of studying and growing in God's Word. Our deep desire to connect with others who believed in the power of prayer and in the study of the Word was a driving force to pull us to these meetings. Looking back, it is easy to see that God was moving us away from our exclusivist mentality into recognizing that other born again believers were also part of His church. In this way, we were learning to look past outward symbols of Christianity, such as clothes and hair styles.

During this second year, God continued to speak in and through us, and we tried very hard to listen and obey. An example is as follows: I was in the local grocery store one day, standing at the meat counter while the butcher filled orders when I noticed that I stood next to a hippie couple, a man and a woman with long hair, beads, sandals and layers of clothing, with their baby snuggled in a back-pack. This was not unusual during the '70's, although in the small hometown in which we lived, it definitely caught our attention. We made eye contact, smiled at each other and I said, "Doesn't everything look good when you're hungry?" to which he replied, "It sure does." We made small talk and suddenly I felt the Spirit of God speak to my heart, "Invite this couple to your home." Within my heart I immediately began to argue with God. You don't invite people you don't know, people you see in the grocery store, to your home, I thought. What is going on! I wondered—Should I? Could I actually do this?

We continued to visit, and as I got my order filled and walked to the produce department, His message came again—"Didn't you hear me? I said, 'Invite these people to your home." It was a clear message, and I finally said, "Alright, IF they are directly in front of me when I get to the check-out stand, I will." After all, what was the chance of that happening!

That was easy to promise but hard to do, because in fact, that is exactly where they were, just ahead of me at the counter. Again I argued with God while they paid for their groceries, turned to walk out, and as they did so, gave me the "peace sign," (like what was I supposed to do with that!!) and left the store. This is when I felt the Spirit's voice inside and knew I had been disobedient. Very I quickly I promised the Lord, "If they're on the sidewalk outside, Lord, I will." But while I was arguing with God, they had disappeared. In fact, they were nowhere to be seen, even though I looked up and down the street. Of course I said to myself, "Aha! That HAD to have been my imagination." But deep inside, this experience was so real that I couldn't ignore it.

On the way home, I stopped to borrow a dress pattern from a friend and happened to mention to her, "I don't know why, but I can't get this hippie couple I met in the grocery store out of my mind," and I explained my meeting at the store with them, even as I walked out the door. She grabbed my hand and pulled me back in, took me to the table where she had a newspaper open to a story of a hippie couple who had traveled the John Muir trail from L.A. to this area. They had given birth to their first child while on the trail. She asked, "Could these be the people?" and there was a photo and a story about them in the paper, with an address and their names at the end of the article. "Yes," I said "that is them," and she gave me the newspaper to take home.

This seemed too much of a "divine appointment" to ignore, and very soon I wrote a short note telling them we had met in the grocery story, and at that time I felt I wanted to invite them to our home but was unable to say the words. I now would like to issue an invitation for a certain evening, and could they possibly come? Two days later the gentleman I'd talked to in the store called from a pay phone at the little country grocery store near their home saying they'd love to come and thought some friends might bring them since they had no car, and could they come too? We were pleased, even though a bit apprehensive, and wondered if we could make them feel at home with us. In the meantime, we also invited another couple, friends of ours, so there were perhaps eight of us sitting around our dining room table ready to get acquainted.

As it turned out, we had a wonderful time learning about them and listening to the various things they had encountered. First of all, they told us that none of their family were believers, and they had come to the Lord through the "Jesus movement," that had originated in Southern California. Soon after their commitment to Jesus they began praying that God would send them some Christian friends who knew more about the walk of faith than they did. We hardly believed that we qualified since our faith walk was also new to us, but we did know for sure that God hears and answers prayers. We also knew that He was perfectly capable of leading His followers in the path He had called them to and to bring stability and growth into their lives.

In addition, they had quite a story as to how they'd gotten to the little town of Livingston. It seems they'd decided to follow the John Muir Trail, which begins somewhere in Southern California and to trust God to meet their needs regarding food and lodging. Even though the woman was several months pregnant they were apparently unconcerned about being out and away from medical care—rather, they believed God would take care of them. In fact, when it came time to give birth, they told us, that "God provided a cave as a shelter for giving birth, and everything had turned out well." They had been given a book by certain friends that provided step by step instructions for the birthing process. They believed that they were in God's hands, and as it turned out, there had been no problems. We were amazed, but most impressed by their strong faith.

It is likely that so many years ago, Mary and Joseph, who had just arrived in Bethlehem, also had to figure out just how they would give birth in a stable, and Baby Jesus arrived with no apparent trauma. God had certainly overseen that miraculous birth.

So it was with this couple who told us everything had gone smoothly as their little son was born normally and was a healthy baby, making them a family of three.

And so we sat around the table eating a simple meal together and talking about the God of the Bible, what He came to do, and how uncomplicated it really is to receive Him into our hearts. We shared our experiences with them as well as many Scriptures that teach us how to walk with Him and to find joy and peace as we learn to trust Him. It truly was a blessed time, and as it began to get late, they asked us, rather hesitantly, if they could use our bathroom to take a bath, since the house they were living in did not have electricity or running water. We were happy to offer them this simple pleasure that so many of us take for granted.

It was perhaps a week or two later that we received a phone call from Richard, our new "hippie" friend, inviting us to their home for a certain evening. "We have the beans on the stove," he said, "please bring a bowl and spoon for each of you." We had asked if we could bring a couple of friends with us for the evening, which they seemed happy for, and we drove the short distance—perhaps three miles, to where they lived. We entered the back door into a small kitchen which contained a stove, a table and two chairs. Then we moved into the only other room, which had no furniture except for a dilapidated lounge chair in the corner. The floor was covered with sleeping bags now opened up for their guests to sit on. We were thrilled that they also had some of their friends who were new Christians, but we were a bit surprised to find an older couple of the Mormon faith who had come to tell us about "the one true church." Since we were still members, although not in good standing, in a different "true church," we wondered how this would go. I no longer remember what this gentleman shared, but as the evening progressed they quietly slipped out the door and left. I suppose they realized we were just an excited group of "Jesus people" and were not interested in learning about a denomination that is also considered a very legalistic one.

What an evening that was! Soon we were singing together some of the choruses that had become so meaningful to us at other prayer meetings, such as "He's the Lord of the earth, He's the Lord of the sea, He's the Lord of you and He's the Lord of me, and He died for my sins, and He gives me liberty, He is Lord of all." But it was a song that was fairly new to us that seemed most important that night. We sang, "I'm so glad Jesus set me free, I'm so glad Jesus set me free, I'm so glad Jesus set me free, singing Glory Hallelujah, Jesus set me free." I was sitting on the floor covered only with a sleeping bag, leaning against the wall next to a young women, newly saved, who was nursing her baby. When we finished the song she leaned over and said, "That song probably doesn't mean as much to you as to me—you have probably never been on drugs and been set free by Jesus, have you?"

"No, I said," I've never been on drugs, but I know what it means to be set free. Bondage is bondage, no matter what form it takes, and we have been set free from religious bondage and are so thankful to Jesus. We have come to understand that it is faith alone in the finished work of Christ on the cross that gives us salvation, and that our works cannot do what faith in His sacrifice on the cross can do for us." Of course, she had no knowledge of the many rules that we were required to follow that made up our church doctrine. She may have noticed that we dressed somewhat differently than they did, but because our focus was on Jesus, that was not an issue.

We had several interactions with this dear couple of new believers God brought into our lives, but then one day we stopped at their home only to find it was empty. It is doubtful we will ever know where they went or why—it is possible the John Muir Trail called them, or that they had simply moved on. We knew that the hippie movement of the late '60's and early '70's was a time of great mobility and that moving from one commune to another was a frequent pattern. For many months we prayed that they would become established in their faith and would grow in knowledge, but in the end, we could only commit them to the Lord.

TRYING TO FIND COMMON GROUND

Chapter Twenty

Controversy, often beneath the surface, continued to be troubling in our church relationship. We had frequent home visits with a variety of ministers, most of whom had nothing to say about the change in our life except to voice disapproval and remind us that to be faithful Christians we needed to keep coming to church and following the doctrines of the forefathers. This we were glad to do, although we did occasionally attend various prayer meetings in the evenings with other believers when we were invited. We did not change our Holdeman lifestyle as far as dress and outward things were concerned. However, as time progressed, fellow church members withdrew from us, not coming to our home nor inviting us to theirs. We missed what had always been the typical fellowship pattern within our denomination. We understood. While on the outside we looked the same, continuing to dress in our usual manner, on the inside we were filled with joy at the reality of Jesus in our lives. We continued Bible reading and prayer, but we were often in awe at the authenticity of God's Word as the Holy Spirit interpreted it during our study time.

One thing that was difficult for us was that when the ministers came to visit, they would ask, we thought with a great deal of skepticism, "Now what is God doing in your life?" We were excited about answers to prayer that we had experienced and would tell them, only to have these experiences fall on deaf ears. Some of these answers were about such simple things, but they always built our faith. For example, my husband was a fulltime farmer at this point in our lives, and he had been asked by the ditch boss to take the water for irrigation on a Sunday. It was important to us to be in church on Sundays, so when we remembered that we could pray even about small things, we prayed. We had already learned that there was nothing too big or too small to pray about. God didn't always give us the answer we hoped for, but this time He did. To our amazement, the ditch boss called to tell my husband that plans had changed and we would not be getting the water on Sunday. This was but another reminder that our Lord heard and answered prayer. But when we shared these kinds of answered prayer with our ministers, there was rarely any comment.

During the many visits, we were puzzled by the fact that the ministers never brought their Bibles to show us where we were in error in the Scripture, nor did they volunteer to pray with us at the end of our home discussions. Since we knew prayer was always the path to take, before they left we would ask if we could pray together. They were willing to comply, but invariably they would pray that we would be delivered from deception. It was obvious that they were not supportive of any experience we would share, nor did they accept our testimony of how we felt Jesus was showing us who He was. We felt that He was leading us to stand firm in our faith in Him and that we could safely put our trust in Him alone, even as we continued to follow the pattern of life required by church standards. As I think back, it seems odd that there was never any spiritual admonition regarding what we were doing wrong, nor did they have any suggestions on how we were to change. We were to repent, but of what? It all seemed rather vague. Surely they did not want us to reject Jesus, but we knew that we were to value the "light" or decisions of the ministry above all else.

That winter it was again time for our yearly revival meetings, and we knew that we would undergo church discipline. The meetings that year had a somewhat different slant than was ordinary—they seemed to focus on the need to place our implicit faith in the church and its doctrines, and to accept what had been handed down by the church fathers as the truth without questions or explanations of any kind.

We attended the meetings every night as expected, and after the first week it was announced there would be a council meeting for members only on that Saturday night. We expected to be on the agenda that evening, which we were. Our case was brought up and was explained to the congregation. They reported that we had been visited frequently during the previous months and that they saw no real change in us, nor a serious attempt to repent. By this time they had identified our problem; we had come under the influence of a "foreign spirit," and that while we talked of loving Jesus with all our hearts, the "fruits of repentance" were not there. They felt there was no indication that we were willing to submit to the request of the ministers who wanted us to publicly admit that we had strayed from the doctrine of the true church. Interestingly enough, we had broken no church rules, that is, any of the conference decisions that are the guidelines for the denomination. However, by simply fellowshipping with non-Holdeman believers in various prayer meetings and testimonial meetings, we had certainly crossed the line. We were hungry for fellowship, particularly since we were being avoided by our own brethren. The congregation took a vote and, as explained in an earlier chapter, we were "placed on repentance," which is the first step toward excommunication. We had expected it; however it was still hard to accept. In our younger years we would never have imagined that we would experience disciplinary action by our brethren.

Throughout the year that followed, we continued to attend church regularly on Sunday mornings; however, we did not always attend the evening service, partly because it was stressful for us to go, and with five children who would need to get up early and go to school the following day, it was beneficial to get them into bed.

We began to get together, often on Friday or Saturday evenings, with two couples who were also being disciplined for not being "grounded on the one true church doctrine," and generally we would have a "pot luck" meal, play some volley ball, and then gather in the living room for a time of singing and prayer. At one point, we had a teacher who was available to teach a series of lessons on the Holy Spirit and how the believer can trust His leading. This friend was a former pastor, who initially felt called to minister to Catholics who were involved in the charismatic prayer movement in their church. He taught a series of classes on the Holy Spirit and talked about how important it is to be filled and led by the Spirit as the New Testament teaches.

It was during one of these times of fellowship that our middle son, Danny, who was twelve at the time, came forward and told the group assembled that he wanted to ask Jesus into his heart. We, his parents, were thrilled, and as a body of believers who had gathered in the home of our friends to praise and worship the Lord, his decision was a joyous gift. We prayed with him and for him as he accepted the Lord as His personal Savior. It was so rewarding to see our children give their hearts to the same Jesus who had touched our lives so personally.

CHALLENGES FOR OUR CHILDREN

Chapter Twenty-One

During this time, our children also experienced stress from the questionable status of our family. After all, their friends were nearly all children of Holdeman Mennonites, and they knew that our family was not in good standing. Our middle son had several close friends whom he enjoyed spending time with, and he would invite them to our home just as they would invite him to theirs. The time came when those invitations were turned down, that is, his friends could no longer visit in our home. However, we made sure that if he was invited to their homes he always had our permission to go. He was about eleven or twelve during this time, and, as with all three of our younger children, did not fully understand the issues involved. However, children are perceptive and know when something has changed. They knew the comfortable social life we had enjoyed with our church people was no longer available. At the same time, we tried to make sure the atmosphere in our home was loving and peaceful as we learned to trust Jesus and grow in Him.

Our middle daughter was in junior high, and she had a number of Holdeman friends with whom she ate lunch. She remembers the day when the group got up and moved away from her as she walked up to join them for lunch. Only one girl, her special friend, seemed uncertain about what to do. This girl had been a "preemie" at birth, and while she had survived a very low birth weight, she was a bit behind in her school activities. Our daughter, with her gentle and sympathetic nature, had become her best friend. On this particular day, as our daughter's friends walked away from her, this special friend was in a quandary, not knowing whether to stay with our daughter or walk away with the other children. After hesitating for quite some time, she decided she should probably stick with the group and walk away with the others.

That wasn't easy for either of them, but the stigma that was placed on our family definitely filtered down to our children. Our two eldest children had given their lives to Christ and had been baptized into the church during previous revival meetings; of course, their status was also in question. Both our son, who was fifteen and our daughter, seventeen, were considered responsible for their own decisions regarding their spiritual standing, and the time would come when they could no longer retain their membership.

By this time our eldest was a senior in high school along with several of her cousins and other Holdeman friends, and being so close to graduating, it seemed there was little time to focus on spiritual controversies. However, one of her teachers, the pastor of the Baptist church in town, somehow heard that some sort of "awakening" had happened in the Nichols home and of course they were very curious. Holdemans did not see Baptists as fellow believers, but this family was impressed to invite us to their home to hear our story. It was wonderful to be accepted and to have others believe that God was at work in our lives. Later, Micki, our seventeen-year-old, would be asked to be the student speaker at the Baccalaureate, the traditional "spiritual" meeting held for high school students a week before graduation. She took the challenge, sharing the hope and promise we have in Christ with her fellow classmates.

Our fifteen-year-old son had several friends in the church, but most of his friends were not at all interested in becoming members, although our son was already baptized. I believe he sat back and watched and tried to process what was going on. When we talked, I asked him what he thought of it all and the stand we were taking. His response was that he believed we were making the right decision and he could see our lives had changed. Looking back, it seems we took advantage of him in that since we needed a baby sitter when we went to prayer meetings, he was ready and willing, and he was always our first choice. Instead of being exposed to the spiritual fellowship we were enjoying, he often watched the younger children at home, thus excluding him from the opportunity for spiritual growth that we and our two older daughters enjoyed.

"The Avoidance" or Shunning

Chapter Twenty-Two

Our two youngest children were still quite young at this time and were quite unaware of what was going on. Our daughter was around seven or eight when we began to be subjected to the rejection that comes with being under discipline and especially excommunication. Our first visit with my husband's family after our membership was severed was at my mother-in-law's home near the church. I had assumed that, being a large group, we would eat buffet style, so I did not prepare my younger children. As we entered the home, I saw that the table had been extended so that twelve people could sit around it, while off to the side was a small table with four plates. Of course, I knew immediately where we would be seated.

And so we were. The card table had four place settings, one each for my husband and myself and our two youngest children. Not exactly what we had planned, but we sat there as directed without comment. Yes, we looked just like everyone else; that is, we wore our Sunday best, which included a home-sewn dress, dark stockings, and a head covering for me, and dress slacks and long-sleeved shirt for my husband. Our two children also looked as they always did—I sewed all of my girls' dresses in various simple styles, and occasionally a shirt for one of my sons, although it was more likely I'd buy their shirts in town. Boys and men did not need to have their clothes sewn to meet the acceptable standards of dress.

This was the first time we'd been set aside and not allowed to eat at the main table while visiting our family, and in honesty, it was very difficult for us. The older children knew about our excommunication and the avoidance that would be expected, but our two youngest children did not. After all, we looked the same as always, attended regularly at the same church as always, and we tried very hard to continue to make things as normal as possible for our younger ones. And while the older children had all fixed their own plates and were sitting in the living room or wherever they chose with cousins their own age, our two youngest sat with us.

However, what happened next was a surprise to me. "Mom," my youngest daughter leaned over and whispered in my ear, "Why are they doing this to us?"

For a moment I caught my breath, wondering how to respond with extended family all around and not wanting to draw attention or cause a disturbance. Immediately I decided to play down the issue, and I whispered in her ear, "Honey, you can see the other table is all full, and weren't they nice to set up a table for us to sit by? Besides, Mama will talk to you about it when we get home."

I have no memory of the rest of the day, other than when I offered to wash dishes after the meal, I was given the opportunity to do so. Perhaps they thought it might take some of the sting away if I would be allowed to do what we always did at family gatherings, work together to clear off the table, put the food away, and wash and dry the dishes. I was thankful for the privilege, but as I washed dishes it seemed odd to me that while I was not allowed to sit at their table, it was considered acceptable for me to wash a big pile of dishes, which, in fact, I greatly appreciated being able to do.

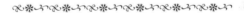

This, however, was not our first experience with the avoidance at a family meal. That had come even earlier at the wedding of my niece, the first wedding in our immediate family since my two brothers and I had married in the '50's. Again, we had attended the service, as we always did, very likely without much thought about how things would develop later. In the Holdeman Mennonite church, weddings are held at their regular Sunday church services, usually on Sunday mornings, but occasionally at the Sunday evening service. This was a morning wedding, and the bride, my niece, was lovely in her pale blue dress, while her handsome groom looked elegant in his store-bought suit with a contrasting white shirt, without a necktie, of course, since that was forbidden. People outside the culture thought it interesting that the groom could go to town and buy a shirt and a suit like non-Holdemans wore, but the bride was required to sew her dress or have it sewn for her by a friend. It was expected to be fabric in some shade of blue, certainly solid color, not printed, and the fabric was not to be "showy." One bride had pushed the limits when she selected material of taffeta, a shiny fabric rarely worn by any Holdeman woman, and was later told that the ministers had nearly refused to marry her. I believe after that experience, the minister's wives were asked to check on the type of fabric the bride chose to make sure that it was acceptable.

However, on this day, both bride and groom wore clothes that were nice-looking but acceptable, and for that matter, so were we. As you may have guessed, clothes are a very important issue with the church body. For example, plain, simple dress patterns are acceptable for women's dresses, as are certain types of fabric and prints. Actually, while it changes over the years, these changes are slow and almost imperceptible. For example, my grandmother on my father's side lived in our home after Grandpa passed away and until her death several years later. She was truly "old school," and was very specific on what kinds of dresses my mother could sew for her. For her, there could be neither collar nor buttons: snap fasteners were the only acceptable closing for the front bodice. Nor did she allow a zipper to be sewn in to create a larger open area at the waist so that the dress could be slipped over her head more easily. If there was a small opening at the waist, it too was closed with snap fasteners. And the fabric either had to be solid color or with a very small and almost unnoticeable print.

But times had changed and there are more choices in fabrics and styles today. On this particular wedding, the bride and groom had complied with the acceptable tradition and everything was in order. At the end of the preaching service, there was an announcement by the minister who would perform the ceremony, to the effect that "if the couple is still of the same mind, they may come forward at this time." In my lifetime, I had never seen either the bride or groom refuse or say they had changed their minds, but nevertheless, they are offered that last minute out.

Ministers today use a little book which has the questions that will be asked, first of the groom, and then of the bride, the traditional questions asked at most weddings, for the most part. One somewhat different question is whether they believe that the Lord has brought them together, which always gets a "yes" answer. Then the bride promises to "love, honor and obey" her husband, while he promises to "cherish and care for her, in sickness and health, for as long as they both shall live." These vows are followed by a prayer of blessing spoken by the presiding minister, after which he tells them "By the power invested in me by the state, I now pronounce you man and wife."

They are now married, but they sit back down on the front bench where they have been seated during the entire service, often with two or three "bridesmaids" who are simply friends or sisters of the bride. These bridesmaids did not walk up the center aisle with the couple, not did the bride come up on the arm of her father, nor does she carry flowers or wear a veil. Rather, the bride and groom, who have been waiting in the foyer for the right moment, walk in together, usually during the second congregational song. It is a special song which the young couple has chosen, and in most cases it is the hymn entitled, "Treat Softly," a tender and melodious hymn. Occasionally the couple may use "Walking in the Sunlight," also a lovely hymn. As they walk down the aisle, they may hold hands or not, depending on how "spiritual" they are. Holding hands before the marriage vow in years past was unacceptable and considered "courtship" because they were still unmarried, but has become more commonplace in recent years.

It is now time for a brief program, which usually consists of a few special songs by singers within the church who sing beautiful four-part harmony. No musical instruments are permitted, of course. Often there will be both a family group and a male quartet, selected by the bride and groom for their wedding. When I was growing up, it was customary to also sing a congregational song from the hymnal called "Love at Home," truly a beautiful hymn, one that reminds everyone what marriage is all about. I suspect it is still sung on occasion.

After the closing prayer, the newly married couple walks to the back of the church to the entrance hall, and there they shake hands with all who wish to congratulate them. After an appropriate time, they make their way to the social hall, usually a large room attached to the back of the church and used ordinarily for Sunday school class rooms by drawing curtains to create small cubicles for each age group of children. On this day, this room has been set up with long tables and chairs, with the "wedding table" featured prominently and with exactly the right number of place settings for the immediate family and the bridesmaids. Other tables are set with paper plates, large pitchers of sweet ice tea, and some of the foods might already be on the table. When everyone is seated, a prayer will be said and then the main dish will be served. This is ordinarily very tasty hot or cold sandwiches, which have been prepared Sunday morning, possibly in the social hall and even while the wedding is taking place. In addition, there are a variety of side dishes, potato salad and jello salad being favorites. In the old days, "baloney sandwiches" were regular fare, but when I got married, my dad did not like them, and so it was decided we would make "sloppy joes" instead, a hot sandwich of beef inside a bun. Of course, most wedding meals include either home baked cakes or pies, provided by members of the congregation. It is a very nice meal, and as you can imagine, takes a lot of effort and preplanning, but the family, the food committee, and other church members are expected to help out.

Wedding celebrations are done very well in the Holdeman church. There is an air of festivity as the crowd gathers. The entire congregation, whether large or small, and any outside visitors are all invited to both the wedding ceremony and the gathering in the social hall immediately following. There may be several table-settings to accommodate the crowd, making sure everyone is fed. This is followed by a time of singing, probably in the main sanctuary, while the gifts are being opened by the bride and groom. Friends and relatives of the bridal pair generally sit along the tables used for the meal and the gifts are passed down the tables for everyone to view. This is a nice time to visit and to admire the household items that will help the new couple set up housekeeping.

Funerals follow a similar pattern, although they are somber and thoughtful, as is proper for the occasion. Weeping is usually done quietly, without excessive emotional show. The singing at funerals can be congregational, but is now done almost exclusively by a choir sitting to the side or on a balcony somewhere. It is always very beautiful.

On the day of my niece's wedding, even though we were self-conscious at having been newly excommunicated, we still blended in quite well. After all, we were dressed like everyone else, we knew all of the guests, the church people with whom we had gone in and out all our lives, and we were familiar with the wedding pattern. However, somehow I had forgotten to prepare myself for the seating arrangement that had been designed for us. I knew we wouldn't be at the wedding table, but neither did I expect to be seated as far off from the wedding party as possible. My husband and I and our youngest two children were led to a table in the distant corner of the room, and there we were seated with other non-members, some of whom had never belonged to the church, and others who had been excommunicated earlier for various reasons. We, of course, were the ones who had been put out of the church for harboring "a foreign spirit," which was still difficult to understand or explain.

As we sat down, I had to try very hard not to give in to unrestrained weeping. After all, this was the first time we had been publicly shunned, and we realized, of course, this would be our regular status if we continued to participate in Holdeman functions. As I sat there with head averted, eyes teary, I felt the Lord saying to me, "Leona, stop feeling sorry for yourself. Do you not know that I was often criticized for eating with "sinners and publicans," by the "pious ones" of my day? Now stop crying and try to share My love with some of the people at the table."

Oh, my! In my state of self-pity I had forgotten that there were others at the table who had also been expelled and possibly did not have the same assurance of salvation that we had. We had the conviction that we were following the Lord by the simple act of being true to His leading in our lives. We had made the decision to follow Jesus no matter where He might lead, and that as His followers, we certainly did not deserve better treatment than He had received. In fact, we never endured rejection even close to the extent that He did. Even though we were excommunicated, the church people still talked to us, smiled at us, asked about our children, and had simple conversations with us about our daily affairs and activities. No one spoke rudely to us nor did they threaten us in any way, all things done to Jesus by the people He loved and had come to save. Nevertheless, it was a difficult experience and we did have a family conversation later as to whether it would be wise to continue to attend Holdeman weddings in the future.

We were very surprised some time later when we attended a funeral of a friend and found that in that situation, different criteria applied. As we followed the line into the social hall for the meal after the funeral, we asked the usher where we should sit, and were surprised when he told us, "Just follow the person ahead of you and sit next to them." Alright! That was easy, but why the big change? Perhaps because there is always a sense of loss and pain when there is a funeral and they wanted to show kindness and sympathy to all people who came to the funeral? I'm really not sure.

Excommunication in Conservative Churches

Chapter Twenty-Three

I am sure that there are many believers today who are unaware that a number of conservative churches still practice excommunication and the avoidance, also called shunning, both principles the Holdemans believe are Biblical. I don't know just what the number of former members is who, through a process of being examined and found lacking in some way, are then expelled and their membership removed, but it is a fairly large group. In the process of being put out of the church, the minister will say, after the individual's life has been "examined" and found lacking and that at this time that particular individual will, having been willfully disobedient, "be given over to Satan" until such a time when they will repent and find grace to once again become part of the true church. If the individual happens to be in attendance at the council meeting, a meeting called for members only, he is asked to leave at this point and remove him or herself from the meeting house.

There are different ways the church will deal with members who are not walking in obedience. For example, if it is a "death sin," there is no leniency given, but that person is excommunicated immediately without the softer step of first "being put on repentance." A death sin would be an extreme disobedience such as adultery, fornication, or a deliberate, intended lie. However, putting the offender "on repentance" is a grace period offered for the individual who has erred in some way but is seeking earnestly to "find himself" and repent of behavior that is inconsistent with the teachings of the church. In our situation, because we sincerely looked for a way that we could stay in the church, the time period of "being on repentance" was quite lengthy. Also, we continued our Holdeman lifestyle and church attendance, so we were "on repentance" for about twelve months. That is longer than the normal grace period given, but since my husband and I were parents of six children, and all of us were faithful in church attendance, the leadership was more lenient. Also, they were reluctant to give up on us.

It was important to us not to be expelled for the wrong reasons, that is, some frivolous misdemeanor such as changing our dress or hair styles, buying a radio, T.V., or camera, going to the movies or the county fair or other "worldly entertainment." For us, Jesus had taken first place in our hearts, and it then became a contest between who was first, our beloved church, or Jesus, our Savior, whom we loved even more. To deny what God had done in our lives seemed impossible to us, particularly as we continued to study God's Word and learn more about what the Bible teaches about walking with Christ and following the leading of the Holy Spirit.

Needless to say, these were difficult days for us in many ways. Then on a Sunday morning in February of 1974, one of the ministers knocked on our door as we were getting ready for church. This was unusual, but we were quite sure what his purpose was. He needed to inform us that the previous evening a meeting had been called and we had been excommunicated for harboring "a foreign spirit." We had known about the pending meeting, but we had chosen instead to attend a different meeting that evening that was focused on the testimony of saving grace by a former "hell's angel," whose experience of coming to know Jesus was truly remarkable. Had we gone to the counsel meeting, we would likely not have been allowed to speak. Our case would have been presented, the vote taken, and we would have been asked to leave. Knowing how difficult that would have been, we chose to attend a meeting that we felt would be encouraging and would honor Jesus.

When our minister came on Sunday morning, he was pleasant and kind, and we received his words in the same manner. We were always thankful, both that day and long afterward, that he also spoke the following words—"We know you love us, and we know we love you, but we just are not in agreement on some major issues." He did not explain just what those issues were, but it seemed to come down to the fact that we were unwilling to accept their evaluation that our life-changing experience was not of Jesus but of the devil. We felt we were sincere in our desire to follow the Lord and to make Him first in our lives in every decision, and numerous answers to prayer had confirmed this decision. After nineteen long months of trying to find a resolution, we accepted the inevitable. At this point, there was nothing left to say on either side other than "Thank you for letting us know." Then our pastor left, and we continued getting ready for church.

We were concerned about our children and wanted their lives on this Sunday morning to continue as normally as possible. After all, they were not the culprits—we were, but their lives would also change as a result of our decision. To be honest, at this point after being under incredible pressure for many months, there was a certain feeling of relief. Trying to be true to what God had shown us without being offensive to the very people we loved was often an ordeal. Our conversations with our people had been shallow and inconsequential for some time. We could not share our hearts with them nor the answers to prayer we had received; neither could we share the insights from our studies of the Scripture. Since we were considered to be "deceived," no one wanted to hear our views on spiritual matters since we were corrupted by a "foreign spirit."

Visits from Well-meaning Brethren

Chapter Twenty-Four

During the time we were "on repentance," there were several significant events that happened in our lives. One was the visitors we received—not many, but a few who cared enough to come and visit and try to show us the error of our ways. Early on was the visit from a beloved nephew who came and sat in our living room, a commitment not easy for him at all. We told him how we believed God was working in our lives, how He had brought us to the moment of truth when He revealed His incredible love to us and some of the answers to prayers we had received. Responding to our testimony from his point of view, he reminded us that being the only one true visible church, there was no room for individual decisions on what it meant to be a Christian. He also insisted, gently and kindly, that submission to the church was the only course of action we should take. Before he left we prayed together, and as he walked out of the door, he said, "I surely hope you won't be disappointed," meaning that we might fail to realize our hope of heaven. We did not doubt his love and concern.

That would be the last time we would see our nephew alive. A few days or weeks later he was involved in a tragic accident in which a falling beam struck his head and took his life. He was a wonderful man, a member of our family, and we were stunned and grieved by his death.

Before that tragic event, in fact, soon after our nephew left, I had a strong impression that the Lord wanted to show me something in the Bible about the word "disappointed." It seemed I was being led to the book of Romans, but try as I might, I could not find the word or phrase I looked for in my King James Bible. We had, by this time, also purchased a more contemporary version of the Bible, The Living Bible, and it was to this version that I felt myself being directed.

It didn't take long to find the word I was looking for. In the ninth chapter of Romans, Paul talks about placing our faith in Jesus alone. He writes, "The Gentiles have been made right with God by faith, even though they were not seeking him. But the Jews, who tried so hard to get right with God by keeping the law, never succeeded. Why not? Because they were trying to get right with God by keeping the law and being good instead of by depending on faith. They stumbled over the great rock in their path. God warned them of this in the Scriptures when He said, "I am placing a stone in Jerusalem that causes people to stumble, and a rock that makes them fall. But anyone who believes in Him will not be disappointed."

Not disappointed! There was our answer. Once again the message seemed clear, that our salvation was not, and never had been, based on doing all the right things, and doing them perfectly. Rather, it was totally based on our faith in the living Son of God, whose great love and forgiveness supersedes our diligent intention to do good things. Certainly it is important to value right living, being kind and forgiving in word and deed, but no matter how hard we work at it, we cannot earn our salvation. The founding fathers of our particular denomination placed strong emphasis on the evidence of "outward apparel." Dressing right, including wearing the right color hose and shoes that were simple and plain, was essential, as well as doing our hair right for females, which included keeping one's hair long and uncut and up under the devotional covering. The head covering, worn daily, was a requirement for all females who became members.

Men had it a bit easier, that is, their clothing blended in with the common people of the day—generally jeans and a button-down shirt for every day, while a suit and plain shirt without a necktie no matter what the occasion, was expected for church. However, this requirement has mellowed with time, so that now dress slacks or even jeans and a shirt with the cuffs rolled up a bit is also acceptable. The important thing for men was the beard, which when I was growing up was to remain almost untouched—possibly with only a small bit of trimming. I remember men whose beards reached to the middle of their chest. This is no longer the case, and most beards tend to be trimmed to look very nice, even fashionable, and to fit in with our current culture, especially those worn by the young men in the church.

One very significant experience we had was a visitation from an out-of-state minister who came to our home to "hear firsthand what was going on." This minister was a friend of my parents, well respected, and one often called out for revival meetings. As a child I remembered he and his wife had been in my parents' home many times. His demeanor toward us was kind and friendly, and as he settled in a comfortable chair in our living room, he asked us if we would tell him just what had happened and why we were in church work. His kindness opened the door for us to lay everything out before him, to leave nothing out.

We began in the beginning and simply told him all that we had experienced, particularly our own encounter with Jesus that night when we had invited friends over and the event turned into a prayer meeting instead of just casual visiting. He listened intently, and at some point began to get tears in his eyes. We told him it had never been our intent to leave our church, and we still could hardly understand why drawing closer to the Lord could possibly be offensive. He responded with some words we have always found a bit difficult to interpret. His reply was, "I don't think the church is ready for your experience at this time. However, don't go too far away from the teachings of your past."

We have pondered this response many times, and have asked others for their interpretation. He seemed to have no difficulty in believing that our revelation of God's all-encompassing love was genuine. He gave us no admonition nor did he tell us that we needed to comply with the church in rejecting what we believed God had revealed to us. I don't know if he was implying that we needed to continue to observe the teachings of the church even though we might be excommunicated, or if he was suggesting that we should stand firm in what God had shown us to be true, which was simply to put Jesus first in our lives while everything else took second place.

We did so appreciate his gentle response to our situation and that his words did not belittle what we believed were God's revelations in our lives. I do know we prayed together before he left, and we were so appreciative of his kind understanding. Looking back, we still wish we had asked him to be more specific, but we were so relived to be treated with such thoughtful consideration that we didn't think to pursue his statement with questions. He was one of two ministers who did not lay the burden of disbelief upon us. The other was a friend of ours from our service days back in our twenties, who also listened to us respectfully and brought no reproof or criticism against us. That was a new experience for us with our Holdeman brethren, to be shown that kind of honesty and openness that made us feel we were being understood. It was wonderful to be listened to without words of condemnation.

GOD SPEAKS THROUGH OUR SON

Chapter Twenty-Five

The final event that I wish to recount was something that happened just before we would be expelled. We were now engaged in the second series of revival meetings since we'd found ourselves in hot water, and having been placed on repentance quite some time before, we knew that we would not make it through these meetings with our membership intact.

One evening after the evening service was over during the current series of revival meetings, our brother-in-law, a minister from another congregation, and his wife, my husband's sister, asked if they could come and talk with us. We welcomed them and quickly put our younger children to bed so our visit would be uninterrupted. The conversation was kind and considerate on both sides of the issue—that is, they did not point the finger and blame us harshly in any way. It was, however, the same message we'd heard many times. They reminded us that our church was the only true church and that for us not to listen and to take a stand against it was unseemly and reckless.

We brought up Scripture that was relevant, as did they, and we talked about how difficult it would be to find another group with which to worship and with whom we could feel at home. After all, we supposed there would not be a group anywhere as sincere and Biblically-based as the Holdeman church. This truly was a concern for us since I was now thirty-eight and my husband was forty, and we had grown up in this spiritual environment all our lives. That fact that nearly all of our children's close friends were in this church also weighted heavily. Furthermore, we had no knowledge of other denominations, nor was there a similar church of Mennonite heritage in our community. We would be greatly challenged in finding a church home.

As I remember that evening, we had a loving conversation, each stating our position but finding little common ground. We ended up crying together and praying together as we continued to reaffirm our conviction that we had experienced a very definite touch of God, and for us to reject His revelation would be a rejection of the Lord Himself. Furthermore, the many answered prayers we'd received could not be ignored.

After our prayer together, they left and we walked slowly to our bedroom. My husband said, "Honey, we need to pray one more time so that we know for sure that we are in God's will. Anyone can be deceived—we can, they can, and God is our only hope."

My reply was a bit feisty, I'll admit, as I replied, "God has continued to lead us in this path as we have prayed again and again. Isn't it an insult to Him to ask the same question one more time?"

"No, Honey," he said—"God understands just how important this is to us."

And so we prayed, one more time—"Lord God, please show us clearly if we are pleasing to you or whether we have missed some turn in the road that we should have taken. We truly want to be in your will" —to which I added, "And Lord, we need to know within twenty-four hours. Please show us your will clearly." By this time the stress we'd experienced because of the conflict we'd dealt with for so long had affected our appetites and sleep patterns. We needed to be out from under the pressure. And after that very specific prayer request we went to bed.

We were a family of eight living in a three-bedroom home, so the crib was always located in the parents' room. Even though our "baby" was now four years old and in a six-year crib, there was literally no other place for him As I remember, we slept well that night, and as morning came, we began to awaken. Neither of us had as yet opened our eyes or began to converse when our son, sleeping in his crib, began to sing, not in his normal voice but as a sleep talker might sound. And as far as we know, it was a song he did not know and had probably never heard, but out of his mouth came these words and melody: "There's a new name written up in glory, and it's mine, oh yes it's mine." Then he was again silent and appeared to still be sleeping.

We lay there in shock, the hair on our arms standing up. As we looked at each other, there were tears in our eyes. We had given birth to six children, all of whom had slept in our room as babies, but not one had awakened singing, and certainly not a song that we ourselves did not sing and with which we were hardly familiar. Our son lay in his bed for a few minutes, then awakened, crawled out of his crib, and went into the hall to turn on the wall heater. He would often enjoy a piece of toast there while he basked in the warmth coming from the wall heater.

We, of course, began to pray together, thanking God for what we were convinced was the affirmation we had prayed for. The message that our names were written in heaven, that we were on the right course, and that we were following God's leading, brought tears to our eyes. We knew that we could not go back and ignore what He had shown us during these very difficult nineteen months. We also knew that having set the wheels of church discipline in motion months ago, it would now be time to culminate the chain of events. We became willing to be excommunicated.

PURGING THE HOLDEMAN CHURCH

Chapter Twenty-Six

Shortly after the church had disciplined our family and two other families in our Holdeman community, a process was initiated that would eventually be designated by those who experienced its consequences as "The Purge." This practice, which the ministers called "paneling," would sweep through the churches with its scattered congregations throughout the conference. While many of the more cautious ministers were opposed to this process of individual examination on the basis that it had never been part of the church in earlier times, it now became an apparent necessity to discern who might be afflicted with a "foreign spirit." To harbor this spirit was especially insidious since it could not be seen on the outside but was hidden in the heart. The idea was that you could look like a conservative member but yet be contaminated on the inside with strange ideas and an unwillingness to conform.

Our family was a case in point. We had not broken the rules of the church, other than attending prayer meetings outside of our group. We had done this quietly without fanfare and only after we were isolated from of any social interaction within our own group. We appeared to be faithful Holdemans, both in church attendance and in the way we dressed and conducted our lives. We did not break the doctrinal rules regarding our appearance. Willis wore his beard, I wore the devotional covering, both at home and when we went out. For the first time it appeared that one could look like a faithful member, all the while harboring an unclean spirit of some kind. When we first were taken into church work, they had no idea how to identify what had changed us, particularly since we still followed the dress code and were faithful in church attendance. Also, our intention was to remain faithful members; we had no desire to leave the church.

When our case was first brought up, the problem was initially identified as a "sectarian spirit" that had defiled us. Later, it would be referred to as the "West Coast spirit" since there were several families, particularly in Northern California also afflicted, and finally it was simply called "a foreign spirit." The number one symptom was that it seemed to place the emphasis on Jesus instead of the church. Of course, Jesus is a very important part of their doctrine, but one must always submit to the church no matter how you may feel Jesus is leading you. Obedience to the church is paramount, and while "church work" is presented to the congregation for consideration, any vote taken against the "light" of the ministry would be extremely questionable. The ministers take the responsibility of leading the flock very seriously; they would not want to be known as a liberal church or one that was lax in discipline or that tried to push the boundaries. This personal shepherding, with its requirement of submission to the ministry in every situation, is considered another evidence of "the one true visible church."

But if, in spite of outward appearances, there might be something terribly wrong in the heart, it needed to be ferreted out. Hopefully, that would come to light in a meeting with each individual member being questioned alone in the company of several ministers. And so this process was added to the duties of revival ministers, also including the home ministers, and taking place toward the close of the yearly series of revivals. For some people, it was very traumatic. A few especially sensitive women were treated at a mental health institution or had to take medication as a result of this pressure. Husbands and wives were not allowed to be interrogated together, causing several couples to leave the church just on that basis. Husbands who took the charge of protecting their wives seriously, refused to allow them to be questioned without being in attendance. That protective stance did not resonate with the ministry, and there would be immediate excommunication in such cases. Resisting the leading of the ministry is, in most cases, simply not tolerated.

Because we had already been excommunicated, we did not go through what some considered an inquisition, although for those who knew the right answers to give, it was really not a problem. When I asked one brother how he had made it through the panel, he said "I gave them the answers they wanted to hear." I'm confident he wasn't the only one to conclude that by responding with the most conservative church doctrinal statements, they could slide through. I am not sure how many years this practice continued; I suspect not many. Eventually it was decided this practice did more harm than good and it was discontinued. A contributing factor was when it was discovered that some ordained ministers could not pass "the panel."

Connected with this temporary practice was an event that, at least in my lifetime, had not happened before. An entire congregation, with the exception of four families, was excommunicated. This congregation, located in Greeley, Colorado, was led by a well-respected minister who had been a popular revival preacher throughout the conference. He was a fine man, a sincere student of the Word, and lived a life above reproach. However, he had allowed, even encouraged, his church members to begin home Bible studies, a practice that now came into question. For more conservative members, the idea of studying the Bible just as lay people together and without the guidance of an ordained minister was risky. What if they came to different conclusions than the prescribed church doctrine? What if they became prideful and began to think they could walk the Christian walk without the oversight and leadership of an ordained man of God? What if they became deceived?

The writer to the Hebrews speaks distinctly to the change from the Old Covenant to the New Covenant and to the priesthood of all believers. The old system of priests who would make sacrifices for the sins of the people had come to an end. The crucifixion of Christ and the blood spilled at Calvary in our behalf did, in fact, change everything. A new and living way in which the believer could now live under grace, not law, took its place. And best of all, the Spirit of Jesus Himself in the Person of the Holy Spirit would now reside in the hearts of those who would choose to accept His free gift of Salvation. Every prophesy of the Old Testament is graciously fulfilled in Jesus, the long-awaited Messiah, giving every believer the right to enter into the very Presence of God and to receive forgiveness of sin. All of God's promises are fulfilled in Jesus.

> "This is the covenant I will make with the house of Israel after that time, declares the Lord. I will put my laws in their minds and write them on their hearts. I will be their God, and they will be my people. No longer will a man teach his neighbor, or a man his brother, saying, 'Know the Lord,' because they will all

> know me, from the least of them to the greatest. For I
> will forgive their wickedness and will remember their
> sins no more." Hebrews 8:10, 11, 12

But for a church whose value of unity in thought and appearance is of primary importance, this Scripture poses problems. How could every member be given the right to study the Word on their own and possibly not reach the same conclusions made by the conference as a whole?

As leaders in the ministerial ranks of the church became aware of this problem of home Bible studies and heard the enthusiastic testimonies of those involved in studying the Word in an informal setting, they became alarmed. What might this lead to? Individual interpretation? Questions regarding basic doctrines that might cause some to fall away? An unwillingness to submit to the conference as a whole?

As the time for the yearly series of revival meeting drew near again, the group of ministers known as "The Problems Committee" rose up to take action. Instead of allowing the Greeley congregation to choose their own revival ministers, the two brethren who would conduct the meetings were selected for them. Undoubtedly these were two who felt strongly about the risks home Bible studies presented. They were dispatched to preach a series of revivals at the Greeley congregation.

However, after only a couple of meetings, the congregation closed down the meetings and decided the revivalists should go home. I can only imagine the shock waves as this became known throughout the conference that two ministers, selected by The Problems Committee, had been sent home by a local congregation. I am confident that all those involved had the best of intentions, but there was a sharp difference of opinion in how the situation should be dealt with.

I do not know how long it was before the bombshell came—the entire congregation, with the exception of four families, had been excommunicated, not by their own congregation, but by a group of ministers in another state. This decision was made in Kansas, rather than at the congregation under consideration, a very unsettling turn of events. As news filtered through the conference, there were blank looks and much shaking of heads. How could such an event have occurred? Had it been necessary? Had a mistake been made? Could or would it be reversed?

I do not know the details of events that followed, other than the families who remained faithful to the Holdeman church soon moved away to other congregations. Several other families also moved away, believing they could live out their faith in another place without the troubling memories and the reputation of deception. However, the core group of those who remained aligned themselves with the same general Mennonite conference from which John Holdeman had removed himself in the mid-eighteen hundreds when he believed the Mennonites, the mother church, had fallen into decay. I am of the opinion that this re-organized church still continues to faithfully follow the Lord.

If I understand correctly, this method of excommunication later came under severe questioning and many leaders came to believe that they had over-stepped the boundaries. However, as is typical in a church where all the power is contained within the leadership, no apologies or reversal of church work was ever done. The injustice done to the local minister was never reversed, although he suffered greatly and always felt that he might in some way have been responsible. However, his flock, though scattered, continues to hold him in high regard and to grieve over the pain caused to this man of God.

FINDING A NEW CHURCH HOME

Chapter Twenty-Seven

After our excommunication, we awoke to find ourselves in an entirely different position. We now had to make our own choices according to what we saw in the Word of God. Having lived so many years as Holdemans, we truly did not know how to deal with the simple decisions we found ourselves faced with. For example, where should we go to church? We had only known one church and had grown up with the teaching that it was the "only" church of which God approved. Now what! We also had six children whose friendship with cousins and other friends was within this church, so what could and should we do?

In the beginning it was simple—we would just continue to attend the church we had always attended, keeping our children in Sunday school, hoping they would not be estranged from their friends too seriously. But after a number of weeks, it became harder and harder—we did not "fit in," even though we made no changes in our dress or hair styles. Finally the Sunday came when, as we were walking to the door, I felt in my spirit that the Lord was saying, "I brought you out of that—why do you still keep going back?"

My husband was less convinced than I that we needed to make a change, but we did decide to try having church at home. After all, there were eight of us, and perhaps we could have a home Bible study.

I don't remember how long that lasted, but it didn't feel right either. The stern teaching that all other churches were "worldly" and therefore not worthy of our attendance at their services was strongly ingrained. My eldest daughter and I had been involved in Vacation Bible School with the local Lutheran Church and loved being able to work with children in that setting. However, when we attended their service we were unfamiliar with the more liturgical-type service and were also aware that we could not take communion with them, even though they thought of us as fellow believers.

We visited several churches, not feeling that any of them should be our church home, until finally our two older daughters, having been at a Bible study that met in a home in Merced, suggested we try this "home church." We decided to try it, and while their style of worship was very different than we were used to, we felt their love and the authenticity with which they worshiped. The singing was very vigorous, and the minister was unlearned but obviously in love with Jesus. Before he came to the Lord, he had been the town drunk, by his own admission, but through the persistent prayers of his wife, a Godly woman, he had gotten saved and soon began to preach the Gospel.

At this stage of our lives we were desperately in need of love and acceptance from other believers, and so we tried to fit in with this small group of enthusiastic believers. They reached out in love to us when we needed acceptance so badly, and so we aligned ourselves with this group for nearly a year. However, when friends of ours invited us to go with them to visit a church that met in neighboring Turlock at The American Legion Hall, we agreed that they could pick us up and take us with them to visit. Almost immediately we felt at home there, especially when one of the couples invited us the following Sunday for Sunday dinner. This gesture of kindness was so meaningful to us since it was a familiar practice in the church in which we had grown up.

Earlier in our journey we had identified quite strongly with the "Jesus people movement" in that we weren't looking for the right church or the church with the most perfect doctrine—we simply wanted to serve Jesus without the distractions of questionable doctrinal issues. Early on we had come to understand that every believer is a "work in progress," and that more than anything else, we needed to focus with great intensity on the Word of God and to open ourselves to the leading and guiding of the Holy Spirit. This we attempted to do. We had already experienced God's grace in our prayer life; as we prayed in faith believing, God was faithful to answer our prayers. We knew we had not gone down this path out of willful behavior or based on our critical analysis of the church of our childhood. We have never stopped recognizing that there are many wonderful qualities within the Holdeman people, and their focus on the importance of raising families in accordance with God's Word is extremely valuable.

We also were firmly entrenched in the good habits we had acquired through the years, such as regular church attendance and resisting what were generally considered "worldly" habits that we did not want to incorporate into our lives. We loved the simple lifestyle and had no ambitions to become wealthy or famous, not that that was likely. We had both been raised simply and had only the basics when it came to education, so we did not have lofty ambitions to move out into the world to make a name for ourselves.

On the other hand, neither did we feel that we should continue to live the Holdeman lifestyle when it came to dress and things we allowed ourselves to do. I well remember the first time I shocked the local school committee of which I was a part by showing up at a meeting with my hair in a clip and down my back instead of in a bun under my devotional covering. Long, straight hair for women was common in the '70's, and while it was new for me to go out publicly with such an arrangement, it was no different than I had occasionally worn at home, particularly after washing my hair. I also wore a long dress, one that came to my ankles that I had sewn which was also within the current style of the '70's. While my Holdeman friends would have looked askance, it certainly met the criteria of modesty. I remember the startled looks I received and raised eyebrows from others on the committee. I felt the need to explain that we were no longer members of our former church and that we were learning to make our own decisions regarding our attire and our various activities. I also remember telling them that "I want to become all that I was capable of becoming." By this I meant that I wanted to develop whatever talents the Lord had given me without the disapproval of a very conservative church body.

My eldest daughter, who by this time was in the nursing program with intentions to become a Licensed Vocational Nurse, wore her covering to work until she was given a nurse's cap, which then became her acceptable hair style while at work. Both she and I were able to adjust to the simple hair style of just wearing our hair long but without the prayer covering. Our middle and younger daughters had never been members, but also wore their hair in a similar style. So many years ago, when I was still in elementary school, it would have meant so much if I could have groomed my hair similar to my school friends, but now at this stage in my life, it was just a personal decision, not a fashion statement but rather an easy way to fix hair.

The girls in our family, me included, all liked the look of my husband wearing a beard, so it was a shock to us to come home one day from doing errands to find that while we were away, he had become clean-shaven. We protested, saying he looked so nice with a beard and asked why he had chosen to remove it. In fact, it changed his looks and we struggled to get used to his new appearance. However, he told us that he had removed the beard for a purpose—he did not want the Holdeman people to think that this change in our lives was just a whim, but he believed he needed to make a statement to show that he was trying to personally evaluate and decide just what God would have him do. It was an even greater shock for our friends and extended family and convinced them that we had truly chosen to "become worldly," and that we were walking in disobedience to God. We knew that we made every decision by making it a matter of prayer and not out of rebellion. We wanted to live out the New Testament instructions that "they would know we were Christians by our love," not by our dress or hairstyles.

The years that followed were years of learning and growing in what it meant to be a believer in the world in which we lived. Occasionally we would find that teachings of the conservative church of our childhood were in conflict with the principles that we saw in the Word of God, and we wanted always to choose God's way, not the way of tradition. Furthermore, the church that we eventually became a part of was a choice we made because of the sound Biblical teaching we found there, as well as the fellowship of believers, some of whom had also come out of conservative churches. We grew to understand that God doesn't "save churches," rather He saves individuals who come to acknowledge their sins in repentance and turn to Jesus as their Lord and Savior. Therefore we had no desire to be associated with any church who claimed to be "the one true church" and who refused to acknowledge or have fellowship with other born again believers.

We loved the fact that this church practiced an open communion which the pastor would introduce as open to anyone who had given their heart to Jesus and had a sincere desire to faithfully follow Him. And while he might remind us that before we partook we should examine our hearts to see if we harbored any unconfessed sin or rebellion, we did not go through a public "self-examination meeting." In the Holdeman church this was a members meeting in which all members were required to participate before being eligible to partake of communion. The meeting was for members only and was part of the process of "getting ready for communion" following the yearly series of revival meetings. In this meeting it would be expected that everyone would rise in turn and give a self-evaluation of their spiritual health and declare that they were ready, or not, if they felt that way, to partake of communion. They were expected to examine both their motives and their actions to see if they were in harmony with the teachings of the church. After this personal examination, they would publicly state that they were "free to partake." It was also a time to reaffirm their belief in the church as being the only true church. Occasionally someone might feel they were not ready to take this step and would sit down, indicating that their hearts were not at a place to sincerely partake of this sacrament without bringing condemnation on themselves.

While our new church was considered "non-denominational," we do have a Biblical creed as stated in a pamphlet entitled "What We Believe." These would be basic Christian beliefs, such as the inerrancy of the Scriptures, the Virgin birth of Jesus and faith in His claim to be the Son of God, His death and resurrection and His ascension to heaven where He is preparing a place for us. These are all clear Biblical precepts and I cannot imagine any true believer taking a stand against this Biblical creed shared by believers all over the globe. While every Christian should be and would want to be "separate from the world" in attitude and practice, it did not include the emphasis on clothes and hair styles so important to the Holdemans. The goal is always to put Jesus first in all of our decisions and to remember that we are "strangers and pilgrims" in this world and that heaven is our home. The reward we look forward to is ours only the by the redemption received through the shed blood of Jesus on the cross for each one of us.

Church discipline was viewed as following the instructions given in the New Testament teachings of Paul and other apostles who reminded believers to love and care for brothers and sisters in the faith, to admonish when necessary, and to pray fervently for one another. Excommunication, a disciplinary action so often practiced by the Holdeman church and other conservative churches in order to keep the church "pure" was viewed from a different point of view. Certainly, if anyone lived in open disobedience, such a one could not hold a leadership position within the church body. In fact, those within the ranks of church leadership were expected to live lives blameless of open sin and to be ready to receive admonition when needed. However, for those who were not in harmony or were disgruntled in one way or another by decisions made by the leadership, these individuals would usually leave and find a church with which they might be more in harmony. We saw the church as made up of a body of redeemed sinners who, except for the guidance of the Holy Spirit would not be able to remain true to the teachings of the Word. In the flesh, there is always a temptation to sin, in our thoughts if no other way, and it is only the blood of Jesus that cleanses us and keeps us clean. True believers ask Jesus' forgiveness on a daily basis as they strive to be more like Him every day.

As our younger children came to accountability in their own personal life, we were so pleased that they chose to invite Jesus into their lives and to be baptized, according to the Scripture. Their desire to live for Jesus has always been evident, and though none of us live perfect lives, our focus as a family has always been to honor our Lord and Savior. Since we did not have a church rule for many of our decisions, such as going on to attend college or just what constituted modesty and other Christian attributes, we would continually go to the Word for our answers. Our younger children, as they became teens, were committed to attending youth services where topics of special interest to the youth were shared and discussed. The older ones had been active in various Bible studies that were available when they became teens, and all of them knew the expectations that we as parents had for them. We continued to be faithful in church attendance, missing only when away from home on a trip or a family outing.

FROM LEGALISM TO GRACE

Chapter Twenty-Eight

It is now forty years since we were excommunicated from the church of our childhood, and they have been good years of loving and closeness as a family, with only the upsets and occasional challenges of any large family. My husband and I are so incredibly thankful for the grace and mercy with which we are blest by our loving Father every single day. As we walk through our final years, we cannot imagine why God has so honored us to bring us into the freedom of His glorious Gospel and out of legalism. We no longer focus on external appearance and other traditions that have their roots in the traditions of the fathers. In those early days when we were discovering the Word of God without the screen of Holdemanism, we were so impressed with the clear message of one of Paul's books, the Book of Galatians. Even though we had read the entire Bible often in our past, we had simply not understood Paul's message. Now, as we examined this epistle more closely, we were shocked to see how plainly Paul teaches against trying to live under both law and grace. In fact, he clearly states that one cancels the other out, and that one simply cannot live under the law and its many requirements, all the while holding to the Gospel of Grace. Of course, we had always considered "the law" as being only the Jewish law and had never applied it to the complexity of church rules that we had lived under for so long.

We began to see that many of our church rules as Holdemans might have been better served as being called personal preferences, not Biblical standards. Of course, under that name there would have been no power to enforce these doctrines, and the principle of outward unity (everyone looks the same) which is valued so highly would have been compromised from their viewpoint.

However, legalism covers more than just the matter of clothes, hair styles, and beards. For example, the rule against allowing flowers at funerals may well have originated as the desire to keep this event simple and to discourage lavish displays of any kind. There is nothing wrong with simplicity—it is a worthy attribute, but should not be a mandate in regard to such things as flowers at funerals and other personal preferences that have nothing to do with following Christ. We were all "good Holdemens" when my mother unexpectedly died an untimely death in 1961. As a family, we followed this church rule with little question, even though it seemed odd. It was only later that we were struck with the inconsistency of it all. Mom was such a lover of flowers—her flower garden was a source of delight to her and a hobby in which she spent many happy hours, but at her funeral there was not a single flower to be seen. My dad remarked that considering her love for flowers, it seemed strange that they were totally absent at her funeral. It was more than strange—it was unconscionable. How could we have submitted to this rule, still found in the conference decision books today, against all that made sense, particularly in my mother's case?

As I close this account of one family's transformation from legalism to grace, I would like to leave a testimony of our family today. We miss many of our Holdeman friends and wish we could have a more friendly relationship with them. Certainly, we smile and greet each other when we meet in public places, but we do not visit in their homes, nor do they visit us. We have extended family living in the area who are more like casual acquaintances than family. Of course, we can always attend funerals or events such as craft sales and the like, but we are rarely invited to family social functions. For that matter, if we are invited to a family event that includes dinner, we now ask about the seating arrangements before we decide whether or not to go. We are no longer willing to be set at a separate table to eat by ourselves—in such situations we might as well stay home. It is doubtful that the day will come when we would be accepted as fellow-believers. But there will be a day...and what a day that will be!

"There is coming a day when my Savior I shall see, when I look upon His face, the one who saved me by His grace . . ."

As we live out our lives here on earth, we are incredibly thankful that our only hope is in Jesus, the precious Son of God, the One who gave His life for our family as well as other believers around the world. I am also thankful for the Godly home in which I was raised, for the loving parents who brought me to Jesus at a young age, and for the Word of God, always an important part of our family's life and something that gets ever more precious as the days go by. To love Jesus and be loved by

Him is the greatest treasure one can ever know. My mother was a singer who knew nearly every hymn ever written, and these hymns are also my heritage. I stand firmly with the words of this hymn: "My faith looks up to Thee, Thou Lamb of Calvary, Savior Divine; Oh hear me while I pray, take all my guilt away, Nor let me ever stray from Thee aside."

Will we ever be reunited with our beloved Holdeman family? Possibly not this side of heaven, but we do know that all true believers will eventually be at home in Glory. This will include all those who are born again, who are saved by the blood of the Lamb, and whose robes are washed white. We believe that those who rejoice around the throne will be from every tribe and nation, and from every denomination, whether their doctrine is absolutely "correct" or not. Those who put their faith in Jesus alone, not Jesus plus their church membership or legalistic doctrines, will be those He recognizes and invites into the place of rest He has prepared. However, those whose efforts have gone into proving they are "right because of the purity of their doctrine and their rigorous attempts to fulfill church requirements," may hear the words, "Depart from me, I never knew you." The Bible indicates that there will be those who believe that their many good works done in this life will open the gates of heaven for them. They are "good" people—how could they not go to heaven! However, according to Scripture that is not a reason "for the hope that lies within us." Our only hope is in Jesus, and those who have placed their faith in Him, and Him alone, will qualify to sing around the throne some sweet day. The words of this song speak the longing of my heart:

> And when at last I see the face of Jesus
> Before whose image other loves all flee
> And when they crown Him Lord of all, I'll be there
> For this is just what heaven means to me.

I have had many loves in my life, primarily because God has blest us with many opportunities and delightful experiences. My husband and I have enjoyed a stable marriage all these years, and we have now reached sixty-two anniversaries. We were both so thrilled with every precious baby we were privileged to give birth to, every one desired and received as a gift from God. We own our own home and have a farm that supplies income, and while we certainly were never flush with money, we were able to take trips and vacations that are still good memories.

We have been privileged to visit many of the scenic places in this country and have take cruises to both Alaska and Mexico. Both Yosemite Valley and the California coast are less than two hours away, and we have visited both places many times. Since our tastes are simple, our family has always loved the yearly camping trip to the Sierras where we treasured the time spent together enjoying God's wonderful creation. Visiting, telling stories, and singing around the campfire brought so much togetherness. What a delightful memory to treasure as a family. The thrill of seeing the next generations arrive and grow up, our precious grandchildren and now our great-grandchildren, surely is a gracious and undeserved gift from the Lord. We pray that the legacy of faith we received will continue to be passed down as our family grows.

We are part of a Bible-believing church that means so much to us and where we are fed spiritually at every service. Watching our children grow and mature and in turn raise their own children to love Jesus, an evidence that the blessings we receive are to be handed down from one generation to the next. Our youngest son, the one the Lord used to remind us of His love while he was yet a child in his crib, is an associate pastor in the church we attend. The heart for God he had as a child is still evident. We know that even during those difficult years of learning to follow God in spite of letting go of past traditions, we were never abandoned. God kept His hand on our lives and gave us and our children the understanding of what it means to follow Him. "One generation shall commend Your works to another, and shall declare Your mighty acts." Psalm 145:4

I was fifty-three when I graduated from college with a B.A in English, a dream I never expected to fulfill in my Holdeman days. I was able to teach in both public schools and in a Christian school, experiences that were so meaningful for me. I love the classroom, and hope that I have been able to have a positive influence on the precious young people entrusted to my care. I have always loved my students and have done my best to give them the incentive to become lifelong learners.

The joy of family who love and care for us even as we get older brings us great happiness in our declining years. Precious friends who enrich our lives with their love and concern make us feel appreciated and blest. Each of these blessings means so much, but as we look toward to the day when we will enter our heavenly home, we hold on to a very precious living hope. We believe the Bible is true, and that our salvation is not of our own works or merits, but only a gift we receive by faith. It is faith in what Jesus has done for us that makes us eligible, and nothing we have done by our own efforts counts for anything. The words of the old hymn are so precious: "My hope is built on <u>nothing less</u> than Jesus' blood and righteousness; I dare not trust a sweeter frame, but wholly lean on Jesus' name. On Christ the solid Rock I stand, all other ground is sinking sand, all other ground is sinking sand." Amen.

APPENDIX

APPENDIX

Throughout my adult life I have periodically sat down to write out my thoughts regarding my spiritual journey. Some of them have been preserved and I include them here for your perusal. These are the words with which I evaluated the stages of my journey.

THE SEARCH

Who is God? What is He like? Am I, and the things I do, pleasing to him?

These are questions that through the years have greatly concerned the human family, and rightly so. For until we know God, even though in a small measure, we cannot really know ourselves, nor can we gain a proper perspective of the meaning of life. A Christian is appalled at the misuse of life today—wasted years, thoughtless living, meaningless existence, and even the irreplaceable breath of life itself is valued so little that life is taken with little or no thought. And God, who is The Giver of life, how does He feel about it all? How does He feel about me?

I used to think of God as a giant, long-haired patriarch, with furrowed brow and piercing eyes which constantly scanned the earth, watching the sinners. He also had a way of shaking His head and muttering to himself about the terrible things being done on this earth. And I was afraid of this God. I knew that even a small mistake would be instantly noticed and condemned, and that even an error of which I was unaware might send me to an endless and horrible eternity. I just couldn't be careful enough. Anything that I heard or thought might possibly offend Him, I scrupulously avoided, "just in case," I would say. "I don't know if this is wrong, but to be on the safe side, I'll not do it." After all, God does not think like I do, and He might see something wrong about it that I don't see."

And so I was careful to comb my hair straight back—He might think a softer look was frivolous. I wore black stockings because, even though it might not be necessary, God would surely be pleased at my sacrifice of personal feeling. Neither did I dare to have a single picture or knick-knack or anything which I might regard too highly, and thus lower my esteem of God. In fact, in every respect, I was constantly on guard—was I acting, thinking, speaking in an approved manner? Perhaps I shouldn't read that book, look at that magazine, attend that gathering, or speak to that non-Christian for fear of contamination.

God was right and God was just, and His demands must somehow be met. What satisfaction I might need should be derived from having followed His law to the letter.

Then one day I read an article that announced that since God is love, no one will get to heaven who does not truly love Him. Love Him? Did I love God? I'd never really thought about it. Obey Him, yes, fear Him, yes, try to follow His laws in detail, yes, deny any wants or wishes of my own that might possibly not have His approval, yes. But love Him, no. How could I? I had never really felt His love. I'd only known His law. I'd never felt relaxed in His presence, I'd only been afraid. And now I was overwhelmed as I began to comprehend that all that I had done would not provide me with a passport to heaven. I would have to try something else. Love. How did one love God? I didn't know. Now there was a strange absence of any feeling at all. I could not work my way into heaven; neither could I produce a love for God simply by wishing it was there.

And so I began to talk to God, not on His terms, but mine. I said, "God, you made me. You know me, my good points and my faults. And Your Word says that You love me anyway. In fact, You love me even though I am a sinner, and even when I don't love You. If I could get along in life without You, I wouldn't bother You with my needs. But I can't. Furthermore, I am afraid to meet the mystery of death without You there to hold my hand. And so I know that I need You, and I also want to love You and to feel evidence of Your love for me. And I will freely admit that I don't understand You, but I want to learn. So I am opening my heart and mind to You and am expecting You to make some sort of contact. I think that as long as I am truly honest, that as long as I want to learn about You, that You will find a way to guide me. That's all I know to do, God.
The rest is up to you."

I wish I could say that from that moment on, I truly loved God and was conscious of His love for me, but I can't. I can say, though, that our relationship has changed. I am beginning to have confidence in Him and His ability to help me understand Him. I no longer live in fear that in some unthinking way I may offend Him, nor do I live in fear of His punishment. I have come to accept that fact that I am human, and that God knows this, and that is exactly what He wanted me to be. Human. Imperfect. Fallible. Subject to error, and errors I do make. Perhaps I am wrong, but now instead of His displeasure I feel His sympathy. I fall, and He expects me to get up and try again. He is just as sorry about my mistakes as I am, but He's not mad. He would no more cast me away than I would my precious child, even though I am annoyed and impatient at the moment. Furthermore, His patience is immeasurably greater than mine.

This is the point in which I have come in my search. I recognize that it is only a small beginning, but as I look back, progress has been made. And as I look to the future, I wonder what lies ahead. I hope that God will continue to reveal Himself to me. I hope that I will grow to understand Him better. And most of all, I hope that I will be able to say, "God, with all my heart, I love You."

Author's note: I was in my late twenties or early thirties when I wrote this, and it sounds extremely immature to me now. On the other hand, I can see that it was a start. I wonder what happened to my early training of "Jesus loves me this I know, for the Bible tells me so." I believed those words as a young child, but as I grew into legalism, the love part must have faded. I suspect intellectually I knew that God loved me, but the reality of my life focused on following the doctrines of our conservative church and being sure not to mess up. How I must have grieved the loving heart of God.

HERE I STAND

(Written around 1993)

It has been nearly twenty years since my husband and I were excommunicated. These years have seen many changes as our family has grown up, left home, and all except Jon are now married. These have also been years of learning and growth as we have become students of the Word and have tried by the grace of God to become established in the Scriptures. We are admonished to study to show ourselves approved, a worker that is not ashamed of the Gospel of Jesus.

Often we are asked about our faith and why we do not follow the traditions of the elders. I have long wanted to write what I believe and why. This discourse is not intended to criticize or in any way put down the teachings of my youth. Like Paul I would have to say that my early training was truly a "school master to lead me to Christ." For this I will be eternally grateful.

The Bible is a book that tells us about God's intention for the human race and how through Adam we not only sinned, but we have inherited the sin nature. Because of sin we are separated from God, but God loved us so much, and He was unwilling for anyone to perish, so He provided a way of escape from the just rewards of our sin. This way is the person, Jesus Christ, who took upon Himself my sins and the sins of the world and died on the cross that through His substitutionary death we might be saved. He willingly gave His life so that what we could not do for ourselves, He did for us. Salvation becomes ours when we accept His death personally and desire to take on the righteousness of Christ by being born again, so that His righteousness covers us in the eyes of a Holy God who cannot bear to look upon sin.

That is the crux of the Gospel. The Word says that it is a simple Gospel, simple enough that even a child can believe. And yet, for all its simplicity, people all over the world are divided on how to live out that Gospel once it has been received.

I have come to understand that the Bible deals with two kinds of issues, those which are essential to the Christian faith and those which are a matter of tradition or personal conviction. I would like to differentiate between the two.

Essentials of the Christian faith are those doctrines that must be accepted if one is to be born again. They are these: Jesus Christ is God, and even though He became a man that He might die in our place, He has the divine nature of His Father and is Himself divine. He was born by means of a supernatural conception in which the Holy Spirit overshadowed Mary, a mortal also in need of a Savior just as all of us are, and who gave birth to the Son of God. He walked among men for the years of His earthly life, doing good, performing many miracles, and by example, teaching us the way to live. His purpose for life, however, was only fulfilled by His death on the cross, and by His death He "finished" the work He came to do. He was placed in a tomb from which on the third day He arose, and after a few days during which time He appeared to many, He ascended and returned to the Father, where He is seated at the right hand, making intercession for those who believe.

I believe the Bible to be the inerrant Word of God, given to show man's sinfulness and to point to Jesus, God's only remedy for sin. Through Him we can again come into relationship with God the Father, not through works lest any man should boast, but through faith in the finished work of Christ on the cross. And even though we receive Him simply by accepting what He has done for us personally, this faith carries with it the evidence of a renewed mind and a desire to fulfill the work that Christ began. We are commissioned to share the Good News, locally, nationally, and internationally as the life of Christ is lived out in us.

These are the essentials of the Christian faith. One cannot be a Christian without belief in these Biblical doctrines. You cannot believe in many gods, as do the Mormons, or believe that Jesus is really an angel, as do Jehovah's Witnesses. Many cults accept some of these truths but distort others so that there is no Biblical foundation for their views. They do, in fact, teach as doctrines the commandments of men.

Up to this point I would assume that there is little or no difference between you, the reader's belief, and mine. However, at this point, we will have different perceptions. I respect your right to do so, and I wish very much you could also respect my right to be true to my understanding. However, I realize that may not happen.

Besides the essentials of the Christian faith, there are many peripheral issues that spring from one's early training or one's personal interpretation of Scripture. It is paramount that every individual must first of all come to an awareness of his sinful condition and recognize his need for a Savior. He must then come to Christ, open the door of his heart, and invite Him in to be His Lord and Savior. Upon this invitation, the Spirit of the Lord comes in, cleanses his heart, and he becomes a new creature in Christ. Now a new desire is born in him; he now wants to serve the Lord and to please Him in all that he does. How he accomplishes this is in many ways a personal matter, according to Romans fourteen. However, there are certain fruits that result from a Godly life that are specifically outlined in the Word. He forsakes his ungodly ways and submits his life to the direction of the Holy Spirit, which is committed to finishing the work already begun in him. The individual does not finish the work—his part is to submit to the Lord. Neither is the work done instantaneously, but over the period of his life. God is at work within each of us both to will and to do His good pleasure. There is within each true believer the desire to please God and to bring honor to His name.

In the fulfillment of this desire, there is much confusion, resulting from many denominational differences. It was Christ's desire that we all would be one, but as we make doctrines out of personal interpretations of the Scripture, we divide the body of Christ. There is only one body—one Lord, one baptism, one faith, and all born-again believers are members of that Body. Why then is there so much division?

The primary calling of Paul's life was to bring the Gospel to the Gentiles. As he went from country to country, city to city, he was faced with cultures and creeds very different than those of the Jew. It was not his job to make Jews out of his converts; rather, he went "preaching Christ and Him crucified." He presented the essentials of the faith and helped them understand how to live as Christians within their own cultures, as long as it was not in opposition to the Gospel.

Paul, as a circumcised Jew, had the right credentials by which to point to himself as the perfect example of a man pleasing to God. Instead, he said that he had to renounce all of those credentials that he might trust in Christ alone. It was not his membership in the right family, the right religious group, the right training that made him acceptable in God's sight—it was faith alone that justified him.

The same is true today. It is not your membership in the right family, the right religious group, or your early training that makes you acceptable in God's sight—it is faith alone. And it is that truth that causes many to stumble. There is a part of our sin nature that insists that we must earn what we attain. Because of our unworthiness, we must perform certain deeds that will somehow make us worthy. Scripture tells us that it is impossible, that nothing we can do will possibly justify us. It is the blood of Christ alone that justifies us before God, while our own righteousness as nothing more than filthy rags.

The Galatians had a hard time with this principle. They came to Christ through faith, but then sought to prove their faith by the good things they did, by "keeping the law." Paul calls then "foolish." What he means by foolish I'm not sure—did they loose their salvation, or did they simply live life in bondage to Jewish law? In any event, their understanding left them outside of the freedom that Christ came to bring.

What is freedom in Christ? Is it freedom to do whatever you please with no regard for God's Word? Certainly not—it is not a "license to sin." How then do we differentiate between freedom from bondage and freedom from sin?

Paul's letter to the Colossians refers to that problem. Paul says there are certain ordinances that man has devised to prove that he is righteous. These are rules that are sometimes hard to follow, that require a great deal of self-denial, but that have no benefit at all for the individual. Rather, Paul says, these things tend to make him proud. These individuals point to these ordinances as "evidence" that they are saved, that they have a greater understanding of truth than do others.

This is the basis for denominational differences. These may include modes of baptism, grooming, styles of clothing, and a variety of church rules and traditions that define certain denominations and are important to them. These are not essentials of the faith but are in fact "doctrines of men." These are "weights" that are carried by well-meaning individuals that actually detract from the Gospel. These ordinances require the believer who wants to honor the command of the Lord to be a faithful witness must also teach ordinances peculiar to his denomination that set him apart from other born-again believers. He cannot go out "preaching Christ and Him crucified," but will instead preach Christ PLUS another doctrine. Often the unbeliever might be eager to receive Christ but is unable to accept the cultural patterns which accompany the message. This hinders his response to the simple Gospel of Christ.

This, I feel is the fallacy of the Holdeman Mennonite church and is why I can no longer be a part of it. There is nothing wrong with the Mennonite culture as such. There is a great deal of beauty in a simple lifestyle and in rejecting certain conventions that have become commonplace in this society, but when you hold up the traditions of the Mennonite culture and teach them as Gospel, a great disservice is done.

There is still a hunger for the Gospel today, not only in countries far away, but also in our own communities. We need to be actively engaged in sharing our faith, if our faith is the true and living faith presented by the Lord Jesus Christ. We cannot become elitist groups that remove ourselves from the desperate souls around us who need the light of Christ. One is reminded of the Pharisees who held their garments close that they night not be contaminated by the passerby. It is possible that we become so concerned that we retain the "purity" of our denomination that we cannot minister to the needs of those around us. It is the sick, Jesus said, not the well, who need the doctor. It is the leper, the unclean, the prostitute, the helpless and hopeless who need the cure that has healed us. If that cure is packaged so that he cannot receive it, he will die in his sins.

I know how good the Holdeman people are. There is so much that they have to offer. But it is withheld from many because of their insistence that the convert must accept their culture as well as the Christ. Some are able to do this, but many are turned away because of your denominational ordinances. When we cloud the gospel, we become accountable for those who turn away.

In this dissertation I have no desire to justify myself. There is no point since most of you believe I am deceived. However, there is something I would like to ask of you—I wish you could accept that I live as I do because I believe this is what the Bible teaches. I live in the world, but I am not "of the world." My mind is being renewed daily as I apply the Word of God to my life. I am not looking for an easier way." It is, in fact, easier to remain in the culture of your youth, in the pattern of life familiar to you. But I believe that I have been called out of a lifestyle that does in fact teach as doctrine the commandments of men. As such, it teaches false doctrine, just as any church that requires their members to follow church rules that identify that particular denomination but may not be Biblical requirements. Interestingly enough, these rules change somewhat over the years, so what was defined as "righteousness" in years past no longer does.

There is a certain comfort in being part of something that feels safe and familiar. This is, however, false comfort and may lead to one being misled. There are those who do "everything the church asks of them "but have no assurance of salvation when they leave this world. How can they know they are saved when their salvation is based on a Gospel of works, and these works may be as inconsequential as the color of hose and shoes and the pattern or color of your dress? I believe every church should teach the difference between essentials of the faith and cultural patterns or preferences.

How do I close? Perhaps by reaffirming my appreciation for the Godly training I received as a child. My parents loved the Lord and loved each other, and lived their faith to the best of their ability. My mother died saved, not because she lived the Holdeman Mennonite lifestyle but because she trusted Jesus. This is the ONLY basis of my own salvation, and it is upon this truth that I stand. God bless you, and may we continue to share those truths that we have in common and to respect our differences in things not essential to salvation. God is faithful, and whether I am the seeker or you are, His promise is "You will seek Me and find Me, when you seek Me with all your heart." Jeremiah 29:13.

The Offense of My College Education

In 1984, the same year my youngest son started high school, I started college at the local community college. I may never have started without the impetus of my friend Mary, who had gotten saved at our church on Easter Sunday, and had decided that she wanted to get off of welfare and get an education. As she said, "I want to sit on the OTHER side of the desk." I admired her determination, but as I looked at her transportation, a car that ran only occasionally, it seemed a monumental task. How could she attend regularly with a car that rarely worked? I remembered that I had always wanted to take an English class to further my writing skills, and so I said to her, "Let's both go and sign up for two classes on Tuesdays and Thursdays and see if we still have working brains."

This we did, and so we drove together to our classes, feeling very strange in the academic atmosphere at first, but as time went on, loving our course of study more and more. By the end of that first semester, we found we greatly enjoyed being students and wanted to continue.

We took the classes we needed to fulfill our individual interests, and after two years, and a summer school class, we were ready to graduate. When I was selected as the graduation speaker, the local paper sent a reporter out to interview me for an article regarding my return to college after raising six children. My first concern was that nothing be said in the newspaper that would in anyway discredit the church or culture of my past. The reporter was startled. She asked why I thought she might do that, and I said that I didn't want to offend my people in any way.

She thought she was being very careful, but the following paragraph was very offensive. It said: "There are many written and unwritten rules for Mennonites to follow. There are rules which cover everything. It's a close, supportive faith as long as you follow the rules."

When the article was published I thought, "Oh, oh! That's not good."

In a few days, I received a letter from my favorite Holdeman pastor whom I had known and loved for many years. He wrote to say that I had "brought disgrace" upon the church of God and wondered why I would say such things. I replied that I had no intention of saying anything derogatory but neither had I proofread the article. My letter is as follows:

Dear Brother _____,   July 11. 1986

For the last two years I have wanted to write you a little note expressing my love and appreciation to you for your helpful spiritual influence during the years you were my pastor. Outside of my parents, I know of no one who was a more positive influence in my life. Your messages did what the Scripture says they should; you encouraged and edified the flock, building them up in the faith, sharing the Gospel message of salvation, and holding up Jesus as the Author and Finisher of our faith. I have often wanted to express my love for you, and have thought that if either of us should die, I would have wanted you to know how highly I regard you and the blessing you have been in my life.

I don't ever recall a time in my life when I did not want to serve Jesus with all my heart. This is the result of Godly parents. Not only did they teach me the way of salvation, but they walked before me in such a way that they demonstrated the truth they taught. I knew Christianity worked, because I saw it work in them. I feel many children reject what their parents say because they haven't seen it lived out in the home. That may not be true in every case, but it has a great bearing.

In regard to the incident of the newspaper article, I sincerely regret that it was offensive. That was never my intent, and I told Miss Booth, who wrote the article, that I wanted nothing said to reflect negatively upon my background. She assured me that she would be very careful, but I should have known that her interpretation would be different than one growing up in our culture would make. Actually, she called me to check on several items, and I asked her to delete some statements, and to soften some. She was pleased with the job she had done, and assured me it was not derogatory in any way. I am sorry now that I did not insist on proof-reading the entire article.

On the more positive side, a former school teacher called me to say that she wished she had known some of the information in the article as it would have helped her to be a better teacher to Mennonite children had she been more knowledgeable of their beliefs. It made me wonder if it might be well to be more open with the community around us. Surely there is nothing to hide, and openness might well bring better understanding.

I would like to say just a few words by way of explanation regarding my return to school. Of course, you know by the article, that it was always a dream of mine, but one I never expected to fulfill. During the years of early marriage and the raising of my children, I was perfectly content to be home and care for them, and was thankful that I was privileged to do so. However, during those years I continued to read, primarily books with spiritual content, but also child development books and books of general interest. I also enjoyed writing and have written poems, essays, and articles, including Sunday School material for a time. I don't think you need to go to school to be a student; the opportunities are all around us. So when I started in the Fall of '84, I took two classes, primarily to improve my writing skills, and to support a friend who had recently become a Christian, who wanted to get off welfare and become self-supporting. As the farm situation worsened, I began to see that there could be some advantages for my husband and our family if I could bring in some additional income. Jon was in high school now, and even if I attended full time, I would be home when he was. It was then that my desire to teach in the public school system, where many young people need the positive influence of Christian teachers, began to resurface. I feel the Lord has opened the doors, and has given me favor, and unless He closes them, this is the direction I will pursue.

I think often of the Holdeman position on higher education, and how I evaluate my experience the last two years. Of the four semesters I have attended college, there have been few Christian teachers. In only one class, Applied Psychology, did the instructor make a firm declaration of her stand as a Christian. She was very clear about her Christian position, and said openly that Jesus was the center of her life. Her kindness and gentle spirit demonstrated that love and made others want to be like her. She was the exception, not the rule. By far, the majority of professors make no statement of Christianity, and their lives would indicate otherwise. Sometimes they say things in the classroom that make me cringe as I think of the young, impressionable minds that are hearing that garbage. On a few occasions, I have tried to present the Christian point of view openly in class.

On the other hand, I teach the college age group in our church, and therefore get the response of committed young people in a college situation. I am impressed with the strength of their faith, and their ability to discern what is true and what is false. Also, their boldness to stand up and admit their faith openly, both to teachers and fellow students, I find commendable. My conclusion is that the student who is grounded in the Word, whose commitment is genuine, and who is involved regularly in a Biblical church body, and who cover their lives with prayer, can actually become stronger in such a setting. However, the weak, non-committed Christian could easily lose out. We have seen throughout the ages of church history, adversity can strengthen the believer if he is grounded on the Rock, but even a small trial can destroy the uncommitted. College certainly is a testing ground, and should not be undertaken by one who is uncertain about his faith.

(A few days later) That's as far as I got, and in the meantime, the letter lays here. I shall endeavor to finish it today. I had wanted to comment on the Scriptures which you shared with me, but it would make for a very lengthy letter. However, briefly, let me say that I do believe in rules. We've certainly used them in our family, and recognize that the Bible gives definite guidelines about certain things.

However, the theme of Galatians, as I know you know, is liberty in Christ. We are free, not to sin, but to walk in the Spirit, no longer under the yoke of the law, but under the direction of the Holy Spirit. Willis and I seek to be obedient to those commands which clearly identify sinful and detrimental conduct. But we feel it is wrong to isolate ourselves from the very world we seek to save, and to make ourselves so different from them that we have no influence upon them.

In the years we have been out, we have found it isn't clothes or grooming that identifies us as followers of Jesus, but our attitudes and our testimony, which give evidence of the Spirit within. We have had heart-warming opportunities to share our faith to hurting, needy people that would have been closed to us had we remained within the confines of the Holdeman faith. Through my involvement with Women's Aglow, I have had many opportunities to pray with women and see some of them come into the saving knowledge of Jesus, and to experience healing within their own lives and in relationship with others. I know we differ in how the Christian is most effective in expressing his or her faith, but we would agree in purpose. I love Jesus, and I want the whole world to know that He saves, heals, restores and makes whole those with broken lives and broken relationships.

Dear friend, there are so many more things that we agree on than that we disagree on; I hope we will continue to love and appreciate one another. When I die, I want the song sung that expresses so well my feeling, "That's Just What Heaven Means to Me." It says:

"A place where there is no misunderstanding, where from all enmity and strife we're free…"

I don't feel that we have strife, but I am always so sorry that we differ in our interpretation You know, of course, that I accept you as a Christian because you are a born-again believer and are seeking to do the Lord's will. But you cannot accept me, even though the same is true of me, because I am not a member of your church, and I dress and live in a normal way. And so the hurt that we both feel will continue, but I believe our love for each others will also continue. We have no more fellowship with "the world' than you have. People who are not believers do not enjoy our company very long, because our faith shows. We have much more in common with the Holdemans than with non-believers, and the day will come when our differences will pass away.

> And when at last I see the face of my Jesus,
> Before whose image other loves all flee,
> And when they crown Him Lord of all, I'll be there,
> For this is just what heaven means to me."

I love you very much and always will. Again, I apologize for the indiscretion of the article, and if it comes up in conversation, please extend my apologies.

Love, always, Leona

THROUGH JESUS I'M FREE

"Salvation through Jesus," we sing and we say,
"There's naught but His blood that can take sins away."
But then, just because we can't grasp that it's free,
We add this and that as requirements, you see.

"Just faith in his blood, just in Jesus alone…"
It can't be that simple our sins to atone;
No, you must do this, put this on, take that off—
You must not go there, somebody might scoff."

Come! let's make a rule so we know what to do—
How long should your beard be, what color your shoe?
What car should you drive, what job should you hold—
Don't bother to pray, just do as you're told!

Until you're all loaded with do's and with don'ts,
Your mind is all weary with shalls and with won'ts
For our Savior has come, all your burdens to bear,
If you'll yield him your life and let Him take your care.

He'll give you His Spirit to live in your heart,
He'll lead you and guide you and never depart;
Just trust Him, relax, all your turmoil is through,
He'll lead you so gently in what you should do.

Yes, Christ made us free, therefore let us BE free,
Not a license to sin, but rather to be
Conformed to His likeness, like Jesus, God's Son,
Born of His spirit, by love all made one.

Living each moment beneath His control,
Safe in His keeping, mind, body, and soul.
O, praise Him and thank Him, so loving is He,
He died on the cross that we might go free.

Leona Koehn Nichols

"Stand fast therefore in the liberty wherein Christ has made us free, and be not entangled again in the yoke of bondage." Galatians 5:1
(From *Quiet Things, Quiet Places,* a poetry book by Leona Koehn Nichols)

Leona_nichols@yahoo.com